Jan 2015! Culver City CA

My dearest Susan:

The magic of Paris brings the joy of those we love. I thought about you while walking the Champs Elysees and seeing the ancient history in it's St[illegible] culture and beauty.

May you enjoy this beautiful book and may God grant as the opportunity to visit & travel around the world.

Happy new year!

Wishing 2015 be the beginning of the best years of your life.

Much love

Mog

BEST-KEPT SECRETS OF
PARIS

Publisher and Creative Director: Nick Wells
Project Editor and Picture Research: Laura Bulbeck
Art Director: Mike Spender
Layout Design: Mike Spender
Digital Design and Production: Chris Herbert
Copy Editor: Anna Groves
Proofreader: Amanda Leigh
Indexer: Helen Snaith

Special thanks to: Catherine Taylor

12 14 16 15 13

1 3 5 7 9 10 8 6 4 2

FLAME TREE PUBLISHING
Crabtree Hall, Crabtree Lane
Fulham, London SW6 6TY
United Kingdom

www.flametreepublishing.com

Flame Tree Publishing is part of Flame Tree Publishing Ltd

ISBN 978-0-85775-397-7

A CIP record for this book is available from the British Library upon request.

Courtesy of **Alamy** and © the following contributors:
13 J Marshall - Tribaleye Images; 14, 110 Idealink Photography; 23, 159 AA World Travel Library; 24–25 fotogenic; 32–33, 49 Ian Dagnall; 35 Hemis; 40, 100, 112 Geoffrey Taunton; 41 GUIZIOU Franck/Hemis; 53, 173 eddie linssen; 55 Barritt, Peter/SuperStock; 57 Peter Forsberg/EU; 58–59, 90–91, 103, 104–05, 114–15, 132, 156, 170–71 JOHN KELLERMAN; 61 Frank Vetere; 63 David Giral; 65 Kevin George; 66–67 claude thibault; 68 HUGHES Hervé/Hemis; 69, 88 Tibor Bognar; 76 Jean-Baptiste Leroux/Photos 12; 79 ImageGap; 80, 81, 122 Chris Lawrence; 86, 150 ESCUDERO Patrick/Hemis; 87 chris warren/CW Images; 89 Sid Frisby; 94 Carlo Bollo; 96–97, 129 JTB Photo Communications, Inc.; 101 RENAULT Philippe/Hemis; 102, 149, 155 RIEGER Bertrand/Hemis; 111 Peter Forsberg; 113 Zena Elea; 116 Maurice Savage; 119 guichaoua; 120 Fabrizio Ruggeri; 121 Florian Monheim/Bildarchiv Monheim GmbH; 128 Eric James; 130 Alex Segre; 131 PjrTravel; 139 MATTES René/Hemis; 142–43 thierryrambaud.com; 157 SUDRES Jean-Daniel/Hemis; 158 Michael Jenner; 161 Jon Arnold Images Ltd; 164–65 SONNET Sylvain/Hemis; 168, 178 Neville Mountford-Hoare; 172 john norman; 179 Montmartre Paris; 182 Chris Hill/National Geographic Image Collection; 184 John Elk III; 185 Michael Juno; 186 Oote Boe Photography 1

Courtesy of **Photoshot** and © the following contributors:
30 Lamolie Arnaud; 62 Imagebrokers; 95 Hemis; 174 Photoshot; 188–89 JTB

Courtesy of **Shutterstock.com** and © the following contributors:
12 Pierre-Jean Durieu; 15, 84 Pete Hoffman; 16 Stuart Blyth; 17 ImageTeam; 18–19 abadesign; 20 Philip Lange; 21 Rui Saraiva; 22 Loskutnikov; 26 Seet; 27 Florin Cirstoc; 28–29 Stefano Ember; 31 isaxar; 34 Dan Breckwoldt; 36 Ritu Manoj Jethani; 37, 183 F.C.G.; 42–43 Fedor Selivanov; 44 homeros; 45 Franck Boston; 46–47 Styve Reineck; 48 Pecold; 50–51, 133 jan kranendonk; 52 plazas i subiros; 54, 163 dutourdumonde; 56 lotsostock; 60 Ralf Gosch; 64 Manuela Weschke; 70–71 xc; 74–75 David Hughes; 77, 92, 98 bensliman hassan; 78, 118 ErickN; 82–83 Richard A. McGuirk; 85 Claudia Carlsen; 93 Valerie Potapova; 99 Pack-Shot; 106 Gorshkov25; 107 Kirk Peart Professional Imaging; 117 Dan Tautan; 123 Alexnn; 124 rj lerich; 125 Patrick Wang; 126–27 ultimathule; 134–35 Perig; 138 pseudolongino; 140–41 Elena Elisseeva; 144 Renata Sedmakova; 145 Steven Lee; 146–47 junjun; 148, 180 Zoran Karapancev; 151 Nightman1965; 152–53 WDG Photo; 154 Patrick Hermans; 160 Steeve Roche; 162 Cristina CIOCHINA; 169 Matthew Bergheiser; 175 Pontus Edenberg; 176–77 Rachael Russell; 181 lsantilli; 187 Ekaterina Pokrovsky

Every effort has been made to contact copyright holders. We apologize in advance for any omissions and would be pleased to insert the appropriate acknowledgement in subsequent editions of this publication.

Printed in China

BEST-KEPT SECRETS OF
PARIS

Michael Kerrigan

FLAME TREE
PUBLISHING

CONTENTS

INTRODUCTION

'To Paris there are no bounds ...,' wrote Victor Hugo in *Les Misérables*. 'Paris doesn't just make the law: it sets the fashion.... The smoke from its rooftops forms the ideas of the universe.' Quite a claim – and yet not one that seems especially far-fetched to the visitor gazing up in wonder at the Eiffel Tower, gasping at the décor in the Palais Garnier, being moved to reverent awe by the stained glass of Notre Dame or the mosaics of Sacré-Coeur, or simply strolling in the Jardins des Tuileries or the Parc Monceau. To walk up the Champs-Élysées on an afternoon in spring is to feel that you are not just at the heart of Paris, but at the very centre of the world. To feel the weight of the centuries in the Sainte-Chapelle; to amble through the future at La Défense is to realize that this is a city for all time. To see the majesty of the Place de la Concorde – and think about the horror of history; to experience the glamour of the Opéra, the elegance of the Boulevard Saint-Germain, is to appreciate the infinite variety of this great city. To sit at a table in a pavement café in the Place des Vosges, watching the world go by; to saunter down the streets of Montmartre or the Marais, is to understand the extraordinary quality of Paris life.

Every city has an energy. Paris's is artistic, intellectual. The Irish writer James Joyce described it in terms of 'spiritual effort'. There was, he went on (reaching for a most unspiritual image), a 'racecourse tension' you could feel when you woke up each morning; a sense of creative anticipation; an assumption that great things were to be done. Writers and poets have indeed done great things here, and not just French talents like Victor Hugo, Honoré de Balzac and poets like Charles Baudelaire, but the foreigners who have flocked here, from Joyce himself to Ernest Hemingway and Gertrude Stein. Artists from Ingres, David, Delacroix and Poussin to Van Gogh, Chagall and Picasso have made Paris the acknowledged hub of the artistic world. Music, theatre, opera, ballet ... Paris has its place in all their stories, and it simply has no rival when it comes to style and

fashion. The life à la mode is by definition fleeting and faddish, but in Paris, paradoxically, the ephemeral becomes eternal: names like Chanel, St Laurent and Dior have proved enduring.

Paris's centrality is as old as France itself. Until the ninth century, the country was just the western region of the wider empire of the Germanic 'Franks'. In 847, Hugh Capet, a Frankish noble with lands in what was known as the Île de France, became the king of what became a separate realm. His successors in the so-called Capetian line made his capital a major city. By 1108, when Louis VI – or Louis 'the Fat' – ascended the throne, its population stood at 3,000; by 1137, when he died, it had more than doubled. Within a century, it had passed the 100,000 mark. Paris was Europe's first metropolis. A centre of learning and piety under Louis IX in the thirteenth century – the time of the great gothic churches – it became a centre of splendour under Louis XIV in the seventeenth, and of decadence under Louis XVI in the 1770s and 1780s. The sumptuous palaces and ornamental gardens of this period testify to the power – and the grandiose extravagance – of the Bourbon monarchy. By this time, of course, Paris was a centre of sedition too and of the sort of intellectual activity that questioned authority as traditionally conceived. The stage was set for Paris to emerge as the pre-eminent centre of Revolution. The events of 1789 – and the Terror that ensued through the 1790s – made Paris at once an inspiration and a warning to the world. However, the Liberty, Equality and Fraternity for which the people had risen up were soon cut off as ruthlessly as their old oppressors had been guillotined. The rise of the 'Little Corporal', Napoleon Bonaparte, brought tyranny when he crowned himself Emperor in 1801, but many welcomed the stability he imposed at home – not to mention, of course, the glory he won on battlefields abroad.

We talk of the 'French Revolution', but in fact there have been several: the nineteenth century pretty much swinging between revolution and reaction. When Napoleon met his Waterloo in 1815, the coalition of European powers restored the monarchy. Charles X was overthrown by the July Revolution of 1830, but only to make way for another, more constitutionally minded king, Louis Philippe I. He was toppled in his turn by the Revolution of 1848, though the Second Republic lasted only as long as until 1852, when its president, Napoleon I's nephew Louis Napoleon, had himself declared the Emperor Napoleon III. Instituted in 1870, a Third Republic showed more staying power, ending only with the Nazi occupation of the Second World War. It very nearly didn't make it through the year, however: France was forced to agree humiliating terms with the Prussians, who invaded in 1870. That defeat in its turn sparked off the workers' uprising of March 1871. For the two months that followed, Paris was an autonomous 'commune', run on left-wing lines. (The revolutionary impulse in the city is so far from disappearing that it flared up from time to time in the twentieth century too. Noisy protests and even general strikes are something of a tradition. Most notoriously, though, in 1968, students and workers made common cause and briefly turned the Latin Quarter into a battlefield.)

While events like these made the historical headlines, the real story of the nineteenth century was the steady rise in wealth and influence of the bourgeoisie. That rise can be charted in the elegant architecture and the opulent furnishings of the period, all the way through from the 'Empire Style' of Napoleon I's reign through to the Fin de Siècle and such consumer-driven developments as Art Nouveau. It made its mark on Paris more profoundly in the massive programme of rebuilding and remodelling carried out under Georges-Eugène Haussmann during Napoleon III's Second Empire and on into the early years of the Third Republic. The elegant look of so much of central Paris – the long and sweeping avenues of trees, the apartment blocks with their regimented façades and continuous balconies, the co-ordinated public buildings and pretty little public parks – was created at this time. The object was partly political (the big new boulevards were hard to barricade and easy to move troops along), but it was also social and commercial. Haussmann swept away the unsightly, squalid slums from which the poor emerged to offend the more delicately nurtured and from which the criminal element sallied forth to prey on its social superiors. In their stead, he created the kind of environment in which the bourgeoisie could set up home in security and comfort, and in which wealthy wives, now comparatively emancipated financially, could go out shopping with their daughters and take tea and meet their friends in peace. Every avenue had its fashionable shops, but there were also now department stores catering for every conceivable taste or whim. And that's not to mention the new arcades, Aladdin's caves of consumerism, with their achingly chic shops and elegantly cool cafés, all closed in above with curving roofs of iron and glass.

Haussmann's renovation was vast and radical, an urban overhaul of the kind that today would give rise to a furore from conservators concerned about the casualness with which whole historic neighbourhoods were being cleared to make way for the new building. And there's no doubt that much of interest and character must indeed have been demolished, including whole streets and districts which, however old and tatty their condition and however inadequate their amenities, represented an important part of Paris's heritage. Fortunately, we have a sense of what they might have looked like from the modern Marais, a quarter overlooked by Haussmann's planners and, indeed, by generations of developers since. The neighbourhood was allowed to sink slowly into disrepair through the late nineteenth and early twentieth centuries. Not until the post-War period was it 'rediscovered' and – carefully and sensitively – redeveloped. It's now one of Paris's most desirable and appealing areas.

The other obvious objection to Haussmann's scheme is that, in 'improving' Paris, it regimented it, homogenizing what had been a city of infinite variety and imposing bourgeois respectability on what had been a place of wild life. That criticism is justified up to a point: 'Bohemian' Paris was driven to the geographic margins, to places like Montmartre and Montparnasse. There, though, it flourished more extravagantly than ever. In any case, over time, Haussmann's improvements have come to seem inevitable and organic: we can't imagine Paris any other way. They play their part in making the City of Light the place it is today: the last word in sophistication, elegance and beauty, the most seductive city in the world.

This book follows local custom in identifying the different parts of Paris by their numbered *arrondissements*. Introduced by the Revolutionary regime, this system was literally revolutionary because the divisions went around the city in a spiral, hence the name.

D·O·M·SVB·INVOC·S·M·MAGDALENAE
LIBRAIRIE
BOUTIQUE
ICI
REPOSE
UN SOLDAT
FRANÇAIS
MORT
POUR LA PATRIE
1914 · 1918

LOUVRE AND CHAMPS-ÉLYSÉES

Here in the historic heart of Paris the centuries seem to slip away. This is a city for all time and for all humankind. Its majestic palaces, its beautiful gardens, its sweeping boulevards and its stately squares make this whole quarter a collective monument to the magnificence of an ancient monarchy – and to the audacity of the democratic spirit that dared to bring it down. Here kings and queens held sway over a glittering court; here they were toppled and here Terror reigned; from here a great empire was administered.

But neither war nor revolution has been able to sweep away the city's age-old status as the world capital of beauty, glamour, style and sophistication – a status it still possesses to this day. Now a palace of art and culture, the Louvre is as imposing as ever. The Tuileries and Orangerie are no less impressive for being homes to famous paintings rather than royalty. If the French have made an art of simply living, this part of Paris is their masterpiece. These handsome townhouses, these spacious streets, these picturesque cafés, these intimate arcades of shops … could life conceivably be more elegant than this?

PARC MONCEAU

VIIIe Arrondissement

The Duke of Chartres commissioned painter and writer Louis Carrogis Carmontelle to landscape this space in the 1770s. What resulted was not so much a city park as a romantic fantasy. 'You could see there', wrote Girault de Saint-Fargeau, 'every kind of wonder that the imagination might create: Greek and Gothic ruins, tombs, an old crenellated fortress, obelisks, pagodas … grottos, rocks, a stream with an island….' Opened to the nation after the Revolution, it has been popular with Parisians ever since – a wonderfully relaxing place to walk and talk.

ÉGLISE SAINT-AUGUSTIN

VIIIe Arrondissement

Built in the Byzantine style between 1860 and 1871, the Church of Saint-Augustin de Paris formed part of Georges Eugène Haussman's refurbishment of the French capital. This area had been a slum, populated – as its name 'Little Poland' suggested – by immigrants. Now a major road-junction, it had to be fitted out with an appropriately imposing monument: the church is some 100 m (328 ft) long, and its dome rises to 80 m (262 ft) in height. Architect Victor Baltard employed a method of combining steel and stone, which he had pioneered in the building of Les Halles.

MUSÉE NISSIM DE CAMONDO

VIIIe Arrondissement

Capital was king in early twentieth-century France: why wouldn't one of the country's leading bankers have a palace modelled on Marie Antoinette's? In 1912, financier Moïse de Camondo had his ancestral home by the Parc Monceau rebuilt along the lines of the 'let-them-eat-cake'-queen's personal retreat, the *Petit Trianon*, at Versailles. Camondo kept his collection of eighteenth-century art and furniture here. Devastated by the loss of his son Nissim in the First World War, he had his house turned into a museum, dedicated to the young man's memory.

ARC DE TRIOMPHE

Intersection of VIIIe, XVIe and XVIIe Arrondissements

This massive monument commemorates the heroes who gave their lives for France in the wars of the Revolutionary and Napoleonic periods. Its gigantic scale apart (it stands some 50 m (160 ft) high), it is clearly modelled on the triumphal arches of Roman times – more specifically the Arch of Titus, built around 82 AD on the Via Sacra in Rome. Napoleon was himself an emperor by the time construction of the Arc de Triomphe began in 1806: he surely saw it as a memorial to his own triumphs.

TOMB OF THE UNKNOWN SOLDIER

Intersection of VIIIe, XVIe and XVIIe Arrondissements

More than a million French soldiers fell in the First World War. The cemeteries in which they lie are a haunting sight. But all too many men were lost completely, their remains never identified or never found. How was their sacrifice to be recorded? In 1920, one unknown casualty was buried beneath the memorial to France's earlier heroes, in the shade of the Arc de Triomphe. 'Here lies a French soldier who died for the Fatherland 1914–1918,' reads the inscription. A flame has been kept burning here ever since.

AVENUE DES CHAMPS-ÉLYSÉES

VIIIe Arrondissement

The original Elysian Fields were, of course, that paradise to which the souls of the virtuous dead were transported in ancient Greek mythology. Sixteenth-century wags applied the name to an open area west of the city, beyond the Louvre Palace and the Tuileries. The avenue, lined with chestnut trees, was established in the eighteenth century and soon became a favourite place for fashionable strollers. The blessed spirits to be found here now are as likely to be tourists shopping for designer brands or simply taking in the scene.

GRAND PALAIS

VIIIe Arrondissement

This great exhibition hall was built for the Universal Exposition of 1900. It formed part of a larger complex, which included the wonderfully flamboyant Alexandre III Bridge, and is arguably seen to best advantage from across the Seine. Whilst essentially a beautiful barn – a cavernous shed in concrete, steel and glass – the Grand Palais represents something of a culmination for the Beaux Arts style (an extravagantly ornate yet at the same time safely conservative Neoclassical look developed through the nineteenth century by architects of Paris's School of Fine Arts).

PETIT PALAIS

VIIIe Arrondissement

'Little' only by comparison with the Grand Palais it stands beside, this fine building was built as, and remains, an art museum. Paris's municipal collection is here, overlooked by the mass of visitors making their determined way to the Louvre, the Musée d'Orsai and the other great galleries. All that can be said is that they are missing a real treat. Many masterpieces are to be seen here, most from the French nineteenth century (Ingres, Delacroix, Courbet …) but the Renaissance is represented too, and there are exquisite art objects and elegant furniture.

PLACE DE LA CONCORDE

VIIIe Arrondissement

The best of squares, the worst of squares, Charles Dickens might have said: the great contradictions of French history are summed up here. Named for peace and harmony, this ceremonial space immediately to the west of the Tuileries Gardens is incomparably elegant and astoundingly impressive, but it has also been a scene of horror in former times. Here it was that, in the Reign of Terror of the 1790s – a simply horrific spell of history – the Guillotine was installed and over a thousand enemies of the new regime were slaughtered.

OBELISK OF LUXOR

VIIIe Arrondissement

Incongruous as it may seem, the Egyptian obelisk standing at the centre of the Place de la Concorde fits in so well it might always have been there, the whole square designed around its shapely, tapered form. In fact, this monument (standing 23 m (75 ft) tall) is something of a newcomer, having arrived as recently as 1836. Sent by Muhammad Ali Pasha, the Ottoman governor of Egypt, as a gift to France, it was created around 1400 BC for the great temple at Luxor, by the Nile.

MUSÉE DE L'ORANGERIE

Ie Arrondissement

This handsome building squeezed between the Place de la Concorde, the Tuileries Gardens and the River Seine was once quite literally an orangery – a glorified greenhouse for growing oranges. But its light and airy character equips it well for the display of art, specifically for the paintings of the Impressionists. Eight of Monet's famous *Nymphéas* (water lilies) series are to be seen here; the artist himself arranged the museum around this centrepiece. Other attractions include the work of Post-Impressionists like Paul Cézanne, and other modern painters like Matisse, Modigliani, Utrillo and Picasso.

ORANGERIE
Orangerie

JARDIN DES TUILERIES

Ie Arrondissement

An expression of the old aristocratic values in landscape form, these gardens weren't designed to be walked in but to be viewed proprietorially from the windows of the Tuileries Palace. Laid out by André le Nôtre, chief gardener to the 'Sun King', Louis XIV, this vast space seems strangely bare, despite its statues, fountains and lines of trees. Still, its open ways gave a clear run to the angry mob which, on 10 August 1792, rushed the royal palace, forcing Louis XVI and his terrified family to flee.

ARC DE TRIOMPHE DU CARROUSEL

1e Arrondissement

It was soon to be overshadowed by the Arc de Triomphe at the opposite end of the *Voie Triomphale* (Triumphal Way), but it was an imposing monument in its own right. This elaborately ornamented marble structure was built in 1806–08 in celebration of the victories, under Napoleon, which had confirmed imperial France as Europe's foremost military power. Four horses pull a chariot on top of the arch – a copy of the *quadriga* at St Mark's Cathedral, Venice. (Originally, the real thing was used, but this was afterwards returned.)

THE LOUVRE

1e Arrondissement

A witty reply to the Egyptian obelisk across the Tuileries Gardens in the Place de la Concorde, Ieoh Ming Pei's pyramid could hardly be more modern. Built in 1989, this shimmering structure in steel and glass serves not only as an entrance hall and skylight to the Louvre Museum but as a trademark, instantly recognizable around the world. The Chinese-American architect threw caution to the wind in drawing up this design. The context (the courtyard of a seventeenth-century palace) should be wholly unsuitable, but sheer audacity ensures that it fits in here.

PALAIS ROYAL

1e Arrondissement

There was once a real royal palace here. For a while in the 1640s, Louis XIII and his family tired of the Louvre. At the end of the eighteenth century, the complex, with its colonnaded galleries, was redeveloped into what we might now call a mall, with shops and cafés. It was, wrote Louis-Sébastien Mercier, 'a unique point on the globe. Visit London, Amsterdam, Madrid or Vienna, you will see nothing like it. A prisoner could live there without getting bored, and it would be years before he even dreamed of freedom.'

JARDIN DU PALAIS ROYAL

Ie Arrondissement

The Palais Royal garden is among the most elegant and picturesque parks in Paris. However, once its style was rather more raffish; indeed, the novelist Honoré de Balzac described it as a 'squalid bazaar'. Lit by burning torches deep into the small hours, it was lined with wooden galleries, packed with cafés and bars. There were also little stalls selling hats, gloves and other small items of the kind a gentleman might want to buy to win his lady's favour. This was the perfect place for making assignations or for meeting prostitutes.

PLACE DES VICTOIRES

Ie and IIe Arrondissements

Six streets and two arrondissements come together at this elegant circus designed in the 1680s by Jules Hardouin-Mansart – a collection of private mansions integrated into a seamless whole. Louis XIV, sitting proud upon his rearing horse, surveys the scene, the dominant presence in a place built in honour of a series of victories won in the 1670s over Spain, the Dutch Republic and the Holy Roman Empire. This statue was added later: a still more grandiose monument originally stood here, but that was torn down in the violence of the Revolution.

Galerie Vivienne

IIe Arrondissement

France's industrial revolution lagged a little behind Britain's, but by the nineteenth century it was most definitely under way. With it came a new consumerism and a new and increasingly fashion-conscious bourgeoisie. Less socially secure, and so more staid, this new elite shunned such fleshpots as the Palais Royal, which went into decline. From its opening in 1826, the Galerie Vivienne offered a safe – and even uplifting – environment for wealthy ladies and girls to do a little light shopping in between taking tea and coffee with their friends.

LIBRAIRIE ANCIENNE & MODERNE
RELIURE

PLACE VENDÔME

Ier Arrondissement

The ultimate Parisian square, the Place Vendôme is a symphony in space, symmetry and line. It dates back to the end of the seventeenth century, and has never been surpassed. The original conception was Jules Hardouin-Mansart's, and even now it takes one's breath away. Napoleon added the monument at the centre – his new take on Trajan's Column, Rome. Carved with scenes from the French Emperor's Austerlitz campaign in a spiralling frieze, this may be boastful and self-aggrandizing in its subject-matter, but it's discreetly done and only completes the beauty of the whole.

FOOD SHOPS ON THE PLACE DE LA MADELEINE

VIIIe Arrondissement

Food for the French is art, science, poetry and passion all rolled into one. It matters how it's prepared, presented, served and eaten and, of course, how it's displayed and sold. Only the finest and freshest produce is accepted and suppliers go to the utmost trouble to keep the customer satisfied. Fruit is sold ripe and ready to eat – even if that creates extra trouble and expense for the distributor. Packaging is regarded as – at best – a necessary evil: there's far less of it to be seen here than in Anglo-Saxon supermarkets.

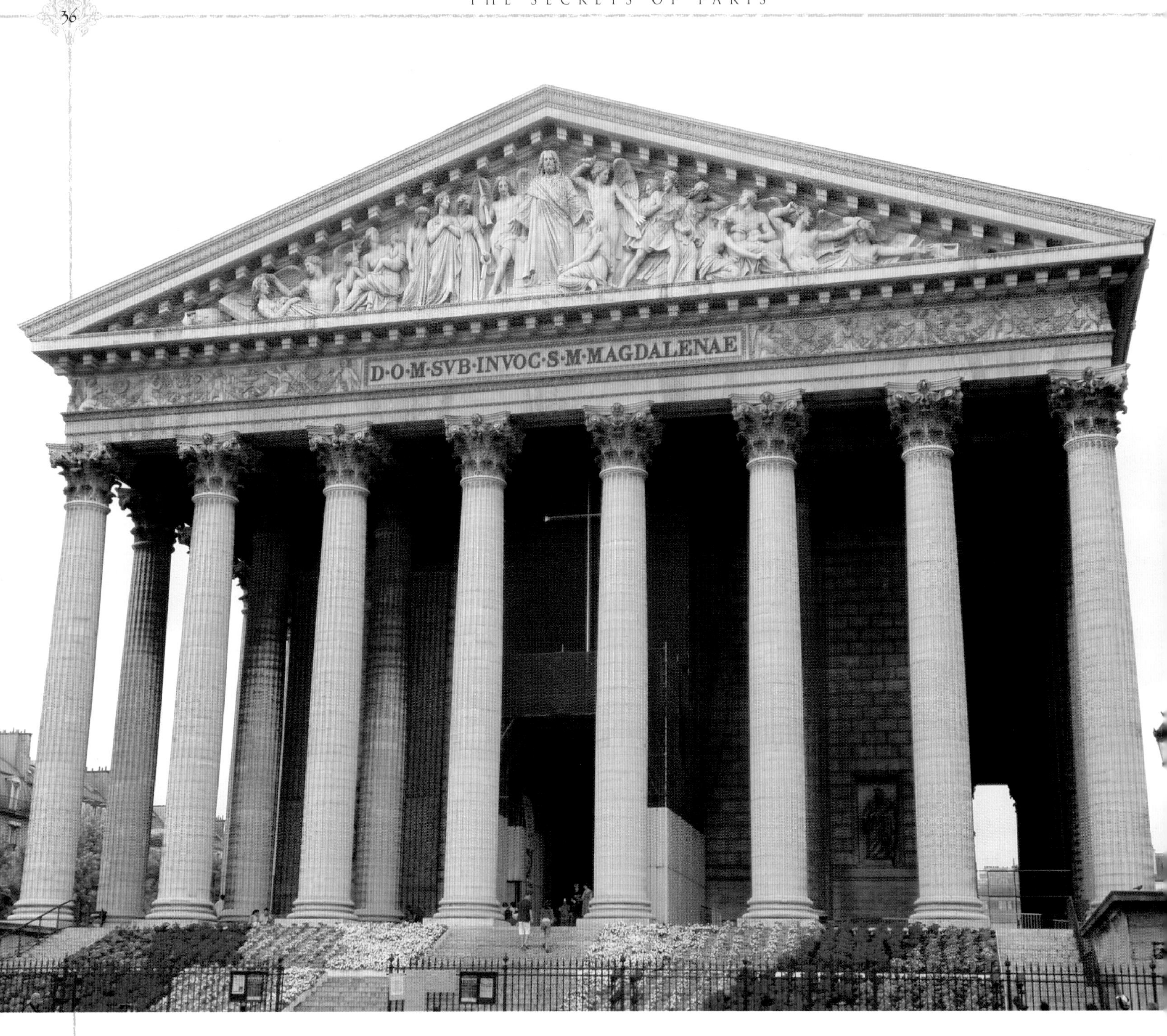
D·O·M·SVB·INVOC·S·M·MAGDALENAE

ÉGLISE DE LA MADELEINE

VIIIe Arrondissement

This stunning building was begun by Napoleon as a 'temple of glory' for his victorious troops. The Classical construction (modelled on a famous Roman temple in Nîmes) suggested a continuity between the glories of Rome and those of Napoleon's new empire. Mary Magdalen, the repentant prostitute who, in Luke's Gospel, kneels to wash Christ's feet with her tears, has been a key figure in Catholic tradition. It is odd that a figure famous for prostrating herself should have such a glorious church dedicated to her, but that's just another Parisian paradox.

PALAIS GARNIER

IXe Arrondissement

'I call architecture frozen music,' said Goethe an extravagant suggestion, it has been thought. Yet in Charles Garnier's Paris Opéra – opened in 1875 when the architect was only 35 years old – all the arts are fused. In the auditorium, the sound of the singers, the lushness of the orchestra, décor so luxurious you feel you could almost sink into it; in the galleries, the shimmering lightshow of ladies' dresses reflected in vast and twinkling chandeliers of gilt and crystal reflected in their turn in the floor-to-ceiling mirrors on the walls.

LES HALLES, LE MARAIS AND BASTILLE

Walk eastward from the Louvre or the Palais Royal and you quickly find yourself in another city, altogether different in its character and tone. This is the people's Paris: while the great drama of history was being acted out in all its tragedy and farce, whilst fashionable society was posing and strutting in its salons, assembly rooms and opera houses, the real life of the city was going on.

Mundane, perhaps, yet the passage of time has conferred a special glamour on these workaday streets where craftsmen and craftswomen toiled at their trades; where shopkeepers and stallholders sold their wares. This was a world, a society unto itself: wealthy merchants set up in substantial houses, whilst poor seamstresses slaved away in attic rooms. A place of trade and commerce, tough and cruel sometimes, this was a place for resilience and resourcefulness – qualities evident in the recent history of these neighbourhoods. Long neglected and run down, they've been rediscovered and redeveloped in the decades since the Second World War. Now they're among the liveliest, and most interesting, parts of Paris. Museums and malls, street markets, bohemian cafés, fancy bars and fashionable boutiques: there's something new and different around every corner.

MUSÉE DES ARTS ET MÉTIERS

IIIe Arrondissement

'*Écrasez l'infâme!*' ('Crush the infamy') wrote a fiery – if vague – Voltaire. He seems to have been referring to the accumulated centuries of custom and superstition he wanted to see swept away. A sizeable *tranche* of French history can be summed up in the changing fortunes of Saint-Martin-des-Champs. The abandoned medieval abbey was pressed into the service of Reason and the Enlightenment when it was made into a science museum in 1794. The twelfth-century church building forms the nucleus of an impressive museum illustrating every aspect of science and industry in France.

FORUM DES HALLES

Ie Arrondissement

This was once the main marketplace for Paris, and so for France. It still is, but in a very different sense. Now there's a big and bustling mall of shops, cafés and cinemas here, and a transport-hub for Paris's bus and Métro system. Not that you'd know that walking at street-level. All you see is a sunken garden with space-age glass-and-steel features, for this little park doubles as a skylight for a multi-storey complex which extends deep into the ground beneath the city.

ÉGLISE SAINT-EUSTACHE

1e Arrondissement

Begun in 1532, construction of St Eustache's was slowed by scarcity of funds. The century it took to build saw a stylistic revolution, so what started out late-Gothic ended up in the Renaissance style. The former prevailed in the overall structure, however: with its high-vaulting interior and flying buttresses, it rivals Notre Dame, but there's an un-medieval restraint about the stonework detail. The western façade as we see it is even later – a fascinating fusion of gothic exuberance and eighteenth-century classicism. This is an extraordinary – and extraordinarily beautiful – church.

BOURSE DE COMMERCE

le Arrondissement

Victor Hugo unkindly compared it with a jockey's cap, but the glass-and-iron dome of the Bourse de Commerce was something of a wonder when it was built for what was then Paris's corn exchange in the eighteenth century. Now the building serves as a headquarters for the capital's chamber of commerce. Nearby stands the Medici Column: 31 m (102 ft) high, it has a platform reached by a spiral staircase. Catherine de Médicis, Henri II's Queen, a keen astrologer, had it built in 1574, apparently for viewing the stars.

FONTAINE DES INNOCENTS

le Arrondissement

The Church of the Holy Innocents was demolished and its burial ground closed a couple of years before the Revolution, the cleared space converted into a market square. The fountain which, since the sixteenth century, had stood beside its wall was moved to the centre of this open space. Originally, it had been called the Fountain of the Nymphs; up close you could see these beautiful water maidens (and tritons, male sea gods) in bas-reliefs about the fountain's base, but these have now been moved to the safety of the Louvre.

Fontaine du Palmier

Ie Arrondissement

This impressive fountain in the Place du Châtelet is surmounted by a column, topped in its turn by a winged Victory, holding the laurel wreaths of triumph. Napoleon I had it built in 1806 – one of 15 throughout his capital. Killing two birds with one stone, the Emperor reminded his subjects of his successes in the field of battle whilst also tackling the problem of an inadequate water supply. For, elaborately ornamented as it is, this fountain served a function, and householders would have come here with buckets for their water.

TOUR SAINT-JACQUES

IVe Arrondissement

The church this tower once belonged to was built in the fifteenth century. Generations of pilgrims started out from here for the famous shrine of St Jacques (or James or Iago) at Santiago de Compostela in Spain. Countless cows, sheep and other animals, by contrast, ended their lives' journeys at the slaughterhouses here: hence the church's earlier description as Saint-Jacques-de-la-Boucherie. The main body of the building was torn down in 1802; the orphaned tower, deconsecrated, has since done duty as a weather station.

HÔTEL DE VILLE

IVe Arrondissement

Dating from the seventeenth century, the Hôtel de Ville had to be rebuilt in the 1870s, after the violent ending of the Paris Commune. France's defeat in the Franco-Prussian War caused general disenchantment and disaffection, prompting the so-called Communards to rise up against the state. For two months in the spring of 1871, they ran the city as a socialist republic. As the authorities closed in, they holed up in the Hôtel de Ville, where they had made their headquarters. They burned it down during their desperate last stand.

Centre Georges Pompidou

IVe Arrondissement

For centuries, the artist strove to conceal the craft that went into his or her creations. A successful landscape painting was a window on a lovely scene; a beautiful building hid its functionality behind a fine façade. Postmodernism, impatient with this pretence, saw ingenuity as something to be celebrated. This was the thinking behind the distinctive design of the Pompidou Centre, built in the 1970s to house France's National Museum of Modern Art. Constructed 'inside-out', it has its wiring, its water-pipes, its air-conditioning ducts and other essentials displayed for all to see.

FONTAINE STRAVINSKY

IVe Arrondissement

Husband and wife Jean Tinguely and Niki de Saint Phalle created this his 'n' hers festive fountain in honour of the Russian composer Igor Stravinsky. No monument could convincingly memorialize the electrifying impact of his great works: this one attempts only to suggest their extraordinary unexpectedness and their ready wit. The 'Firebird' (shown here) squirts water from the points of its spiky crest; there's also a fox (for the opera-ballet *Renard*), a nightingale (for the opera *Le Rossignol*) and various figures from the famous ballet *The Rite of Spring*.

LE DÉFENSEUR DU TEMPS

IIIe Arrondissement

This part of Paris has always been a centre for skilled trades, so it's no surprise that it has a Quartier de l'Horloge (Clock Quarter). This is no row of historic houses, though, but a modern development from the 1970s. And the clock in question – created by Jacques Monestier – is as much an artwork as a timepiece, its 'defence of time' symbolic as well as technical. On the hour, the warrior defends the clock against (at different times) a crab, a bird or a dragon, representing the elements of water, air and fire respectively.

HÔTEL DE SOUBISE

IIIe Arrondissement

The Marais, though later a commercial quarter, was for hundreds of years home to the gentry. The great aristocratic families had their houses here. By the seventeenth century, they were starting to drift westward to new suburbs beyond Saint Germain-des-Prés, but some – like the Prince and Princess de Soubise – stayed, buying a house which had belonged to the Dukes of Guise. Between 1700 and 1705, they had it rebuilt in stunning style, all Classical restraint without and Rococo exuberance within. Since 1867 it has housed the Museum of French History.

MUSÉE PICASSO

IIIe Arrondissement

The Hôtel Salé, in the Marais, took its name from the occupation of the man who built it having made his fortune collecting salt-tax in the seventeenth century. Since 1985, it's been dedicated to the memory of the great Catalan painter and sculptor, Pablo Picasso, who made the Paris art scene his own in the early decades of the twentieth century. A marvellous museum, it houses the artist's personal collection – of his own work and that of others he admired, including Braque and Rousseau and earlier works by Cézanne, Dégas and Matisse.

MUSÉE CARNAVALET

IIIe Arrondissement

One of Paris's most appealing and interesting museums, the Carnavalet, in the rue de Sévigné, chronicles the whole history of the city from prehistoric times to the present day. There are dugout canoes dating back more than 6,000 years, along with fascinating items from the medieval, Renaissance and Revolutionary eras, and every period since. The collection is strikingly presented, set off as it is by the sumptuous surroundings of two of the capital's finest former aristocratic houses: the Hôtel de Carnavalet and the Hôtel le Peletier de Saint-Fargeau.

SQUARE GEORGES-CAIN

IIIe Arrondissement

One of a number of small squares scattered through the Marais district, the Square Georges-Cain is the perfect place for a quiet stroll or sit-down. Georges Cain was a writer, artist and – above all – the curator of the nearby Carnavalet Museum, so it's fitting that the square that bears his name should be adorned around its edges with archeological fragments from Paris's past. The statue at the centre – a female nude by Aristide Maillol – is an allegorical representation of the Île de France, the historic French region of which Paris forms the heart.

VILLAGE SAINT-PAUL

IVe Arrondissement

This little neighbourhood in the heart of the Marais may be seen to typify the transformation of the Marais as a whole. A few blocks in what was once the Jewish Quarter, it became a backwater in the latter part of the nineteenth century and, for much of the twentieth, was allowed to go to rack and ruin. In the last few decades, however, its character was rediscovered. It's now a fashionable (and frighteningly expensive) shopping district, and a lovely area in which to walk and browse.

HÔTEL DE SULLY

IVe Arrondissement

This spectacular city mansion was built in the 1620s by a wealthy financier before being bought by Henri IV's Superintendent of Finances, the Duke of Sully, in 1634. A historic monument in its own right, the Hôtel de Sully has since 1967 been the *Centre des monuments nationaux* – the base from which France's whole collection of historic monuments has been administered. As such, it's a working office complex and consequently off-limits to visitors, but the grounds and gardens (including a seventeenth-century orangery) are open to the public, and well worth seeing.

PLACE DES VOSGES

IVe Arrondissement

It would be a pity if the Place des Vosges were known only as one of Paris's swankiest addresses, because the city's oldest square is also one of the loveliest and the most historically interesting. Henri IV had it built as the Place Royale at the beginning of the seventeenth century, its handsome houses all integrated to a single, seamless design. At number 6, the Maison de Victor Hugo is now a museum, devoted to the life and work of the author of *Les Misérables*, who lived here from 1832 to 1848.

ARCADES IN THE PLACE DES VOSGES

IVe Arrondissement

The houses here stand atop columned arcades, ideal for strolling or sitting at cafés, musing, chatting or watching the world go by. The perfect reconciliation of private and public space, this square has witnessed the tug of war between the two spheres. Revolutionary France had no place for a Place Royale, so in 1799 it was renamed in honour of the first *département* to pay its taxes to the new regime. Though the restored monarchy restored the royal name, it was changed back in 1848: it has remained the Place des Vosges ever since.

COUR DAMOYE

XIe Arrondissement

In recent years, Bastille has been very much an up-and-coming area. That's partly because, in what had long been a run-down quarter, young artists were able to find affordably priced industrial lofts they could convert into living- and working-space, following a trend set in New York's SoHo and London's Hoxton. But it's also been a matter of rediscovering the qualities of forgotten little corners like this one, just off the Place de la Bastille. Montmartre or the Marais would be pushed to come up with a scene more picturesque than this.

JULY COLUMN, PLACE DE LA BASTILLE

Intersections of IVe, XIe and XIIe Arrondissements

There's no more famous event in French history than the storming of the Bastille in July 1789, the uprising that set off the Revolution. It is commemorated by an imposing column. Other than this, a glance around the Place de la Bastille reveals a busy road-junction but no obvious trace of the notorious fortress in which the political prisoners were held by the *Ancien Régime*. In fact, in those days before heritage-consciousness, the instinct was immediately to raze the Bastille to the ground. Markers on the pavement show where it once stood.

OPÉRA BASTILLE

XIIe Arrondissement

This building was built in 1989 as a base for the French National Opera; the Palais Garnier didn't offer the flexibility or scope that modern productions needed. It could hardly be more different than its nineteenth-century predecessor. Too different, some have suggested: if Charles Garnier's creation was a wildly extravagant confection, Carlos Ott's design was uncompromisingly sober. Squat in shape, it presents a blank expanse of glass, stone and steel to the world. Inside, though, it's state-of-the-art; perfect in its sightlines and acoustics, it is one of the pre-eminent performance venues in the world.

OPERA
130, rue de Lyon

PROMENADE PLANTÉE

XIIe Arrondissement

Starting just to the south of the Opéra Bastille, this beautifully landscaped walkway runs eastward for a distance of almost 5 km (3 miles), ending in the shadow of the Boulevard Périphérique or Paris ring-road. A haven of calm and colour, for much of its length it is elevated several metres above the surrounding city, offering exciting views across the east of Paris. Created in the 1980s, the Promenade Plantée followed the route of a suburban railway line, which closed in 1969. It has been the inspiration for similar schemes worldwide.

PASSAGE LHOMME

XIe Arrondissement

Among Paris's best-kept secrets are the numerous 'passages' – little lanes, more alleys than streets – to be found tucked away around odd corners in the Faubourg Saint-Antoine. Among the most characterful is the Passage Lhomme. This part of Paris was for a long time a centre for the furniture trade, and it is home to this day to artisans in cabinetmaking and carpentry. Gradually, though, it has been 'gentrifying': the tradesmen's *ateliers* giving way to trendy shops and cafés; their living accommodation to the city's more moneyed and fashion-conscious young.

PLACE DE LA RÉPUBLIQUE

Between the IIIe, Xe and XIe Arrondissements

Ironically enough, the Place de la République as we now know it was the product of Napoleon III's Second Empire. Georges-Eugène Haussmann's plan for Paris is generally held to have been a big success and this square is undeniably handsome, but its construction came at the cost of one of the Marais' most interesting districts. Beside the Boulevard du Temple was a lively theatreland, with characterful old buildings. During *Les Événements* of May 1968, 200,000 protesting students and striking workers mustered in the Place before their climactic march on the Left Bank.

Apelco

PORT DE PLAISANCE DE PARIS-ARSENAL

Between IVe and XIIe Arrondissements

Just to the south of the Place de la Bastille, by the site of the old Arsenal, is a lively marina bustling with boats all year round. Now an integrated part of the national canal system, the Bassin de l'Arsenal was once a reservoir storing the water needed to keep up the levels of the moat around the Bastille. Deepened in the nineteenth century, it handled commercial traffic, connecting Paris's canals with the River Seine. Since 1983, it has been given over exclusively to pleasure craft.

THE ISLANDS AND THE OUTSKIRTS

To travel from the Île de la Cité to La Défense is to take a trip in time, from Paris past to Paris future, from origins to outcomes. France's capital had its first beginnings on the island, which is still the historic and spiritual heart of the modern city. It forges ahead at a new frontier beyond the *Périphérique*, Paris's ring-road.

The contrast couldn't be starker now: medieval Cité (and the adjacent Île Saint-Louis, laid out in the seventeenth century) feel like islands not just geographically – or even historically – but, in their calm and quiet atmosphere of self-containment, psychologically as well. Places apart, they seem secluded from present reality, far removed from the fuss and bustle of the twenty-first-century city. Out at La Défense it's different: this is Paris at the cutting edge, but there's much more to these outer areas than future-shock. This part of Paris has a history of its own, and has its own sanctuaries of peace in its parks and cemeteries. After all, for centuries Parisians fled here precisely to escape from the centre of their city; the serenity they sought can still be found today.

ÎLE DE LA CITÉ AND PONT NEUF

Ie and IVe Arrondissements

It is easy enough to see why an ancient Celtic tribe should have wanted to establish themselves here in the third century BC, safe and secure on an island in the middle of the Seine.

Fishermen, farmers and warriors, the Parisii enjoyed advantages in all these spheres. They were also well placed to trade with communities up and downriver. Ironically, the oldest bridge in Paris, the Pont Neuf, was built in the sixteenth century, though it was at that time 'new' by comparison with the existing version of the Pont Notre-Dame.

SQUARE DU VERT-GALANT

le Arrondissement

Henri IV was the original 'Green Gallant'. France's king from 1589 to 1610, he remained both fresh in spirit and fresh with the ladies well into what should have been his declining years. As green as the monarch for which it was named, this appealing little park at the Île de la Cité's downstream end is a lovely place in which to walk or rest, and from which to look out across the Seine to the Pont Neuf, northward to the Louvre or south to the Hôtel des Monnaies or Mint.

PLACE DAUPHINE

le Arrondissement

From the fourteenth century, the title *dauphin* was conferred upon the heir apparent to the throne of France, the word referring to the heraldic dolphin on his royal coat of arms. When what had been a patch of waste ground was developed into this splendid square (well, in truth it's a triangle), Henri IV dedicated it to his young son, who had been born just a few years earlier in 1601. The boy wasn't destined to be Dauphin for long: Henri died in 1610 and his son ascended the throne as Louis XIII.

THE CONCIERGERIE

1e Arrondissement

Such was the majesty of medieval France and its monarchy that the palace concierge, or caretaker, had a palace of his own. In fact, French kings and queens had lived in it themselves from the tenth to the fourteenth century, leaving this one vacant when they crossed the river to the Louvre. When the monarchy fell, inevitably, the royal Conciergerie changed its function, being given over to good housekeeping of a grimmer kind. Here it was that enemies of the revolutionary regime were incarcerated before they made their final journey to the Guillotine.

SAINTE-CHAPELLE

1e Arrondissement

Richly jewelled caskets were made for the sacred relics that the Middle Ages prized so fervently. Louis IX – Saint Louis – built this 'holy chapel' as a vast reliquary in glass and stone. He had just spent a fortune on a fragment of Christ's 'True Cross', and the Crown of Thorns, which had been used to mock him as he died. Those relics have been lost in the centuries since, but the Sainte-Chapelle (seen here to the left) still inspires awe with its thorn-like gothic spire and spikes, its stunning stained-glass windows and its opulently decorated interior.

LES DEUX PALAIS

MARCHÉ AUX FLEURS

IVe Arrondissement

The Flower Market on the Place Louis Lépine is one of Paris's best-kept secrets but a truly delightful one. It comes as a complete surprise to the afternoon ambler on the Île de la Cité. To wander down its arcaded aisles is to be overwhelmed, to be enfolded by a quiet explosion of fragrance and colour. And not necessarily so quiet, given the cacophony of chirping, cawing, twittering and whistling song which erupts on Sundays, for on that day, caged birds are sold as well.

RESTAURANT ON THE RUE CHANOINESSE

IVe Arrondissement

Even in the Île de la Cité, medieval Paris has mostly been swept away, but in a couple of small pockets, the ancient street plan has been preserved. One of these is around the rue Chanoinesse, which runs to the east of Notre Dame, between the Cathedral and the River Seine. Once, of course, this quarter would have been full of bustling life; now it's a great deal quieter, more select – a place of smart restaurants and even smarter apartments. Even so, it still has a very special feel.

Au Vieux Paris
Auberge depuis 1794
AU VIEUX PARIS

NOTRE DAME

IVe Arrondissement

The ultimate in Gothic architecture, an acknowledged high point in medieval art, the Cathedral of Our Lady was built in the second half of the twelfth century. Between the twin towers of its west front (visible, left) is a celebrated rose window; taken together with the arched windows which line the nave on either side, the result is a veritable symphony in stained glass. Once you've explored the cathedral itself, climb the spiral staircase to the top of the tower and enjoy spectacular views over the city of Paris.

NOTRE DAME, GARGOYLE AND VIEW FROM NORTH TOWER

IVe Arrondissement

Though it's held in reverence now – even by non-believers – as a vital part of Parisian heritage and identity, Notre Dame wasn't always treasured. Whilst the Renaissance and Enlightenment had disdained the 'barbarities' of medieval art, the Revolution rejected religious 'superstitions' and this great church was allowed to fall into ruin. But the Romantic movement's rediscovery of a 'gothic' sensibility of ghouls, ghosts and monstrous passions led to its rediscovery. Furthermore, Victor Hugo's novel *Notre Dame de Paris* – with its famous hunchback – put the cathedral right back on the map.

SQUARE JEAN XXIII

IVe Arrondissement

It's a pleasant enough place in itself, but this little park is chiefly of value as a vantage point for viewing the 'flying buttresses' of Notre Dame's eastern end. The innovation that, along with the pointed arch, made the High Gothic possible, these provided extra structural support, allowing medieval masons to build to greater heights. Since the walls didn't have to do so much work, they could be less massive than they had been and have bigger windows – hence the stained-glass extravaganzas of the Gothic age.

Île Saint-Louis, Quai d'Anjou

IVe Arrondissement

The Cité's neighbouring island, the Île Saint-Louis is essentially a quiet residential quarter in the middle of the Seine. The handsome blocks of the Quai d'Anjou (on the eastern side) are typical. Sedate as it may now seem, this neighbourhood once had a distinctly bohemian feel: during the nineteenth century, several sculptors and painters (including Paul Cézanne) set up here. The Quai d'Anjou itself was home to self-consciously decadent poets like Théophile Gautier and Charles Baudelaire, whose *Fleurs du Mal* (Flowers of Evil) took the world of literature by storm in 1857.

Saint-Louis Street Scene

IVe Arrondissement

It says something about the diminutive scale on which the island is laid out that the rue Saint-Louis en l'Île is its main thoroughfare. Running right down the middle from one end to the other, it is the island's east–west axis, though it's little more than a lane by any normal standards. Shops, restaurants and cafés crowd its length. The street has become a popular place for the more discriminating (and affluent) tourist precisely because it's succeeded in holding on to so much of its old-world character and charm.

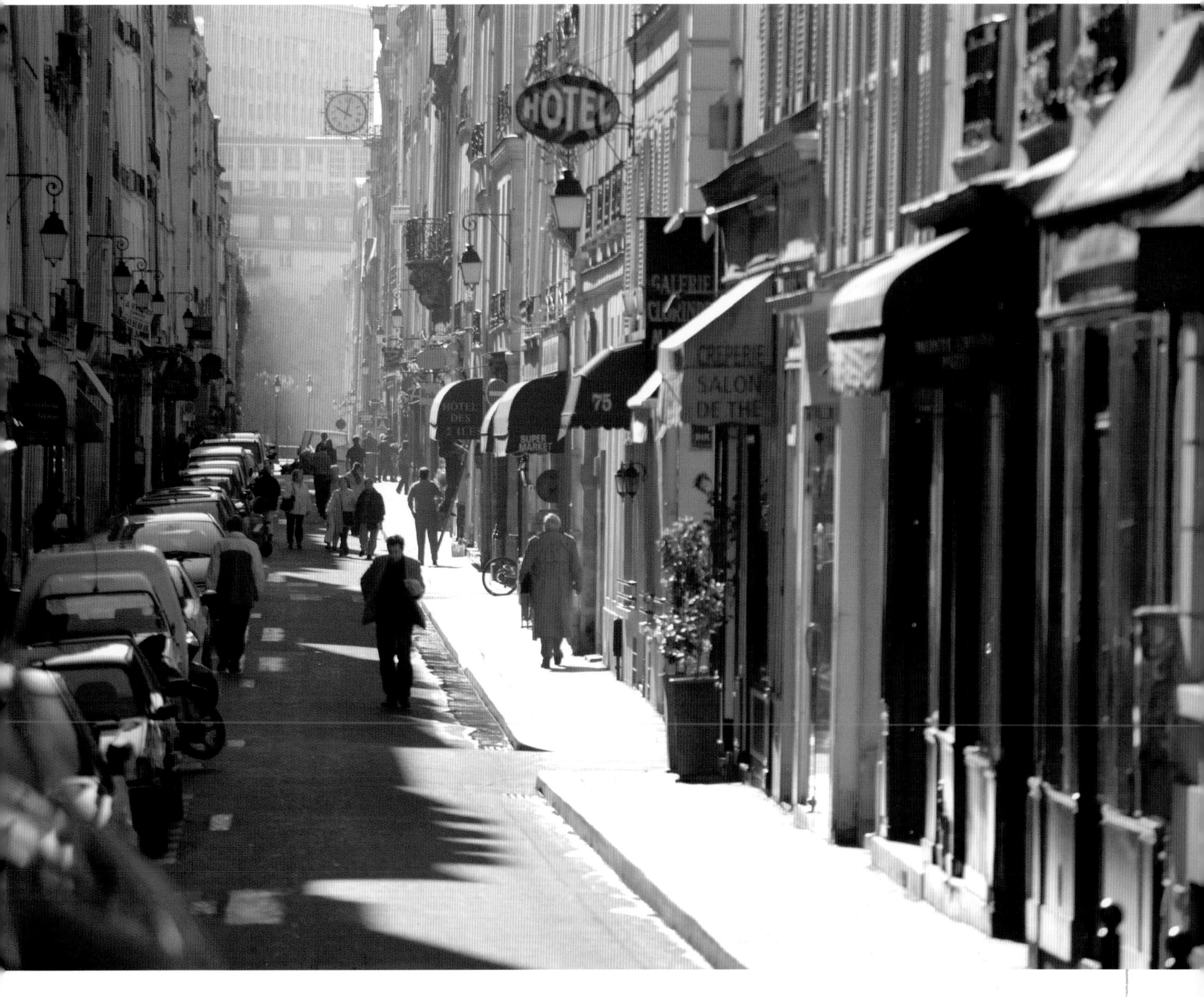
HOTEL
GALERIE
75
SUPER MARKET
CREPERIE
SALON
DE THE

SQUARE BARYE

IVe Arrondissement

This triangular 'square' occupies the eastern tip of the Île Saint-Louis. It is bounded on one side by the Pont Sully; on two sides by the Seine itself. Viewed from upriver, at least in the summer months, all that can be seen is an eruption of greenery from its wooded walks. A shady refuge from the sun and heat, the square has a wonderfully intimate feel. Once the garden for the nearby Hôtel de Bretonvilliers, it is now a public park. It has a monument to the sculptor Antoine-Louis Barye (1796–1875).

PARC DE LA VILLETTE, CAROUSEL

XIXe Arrondissement

Just a few kilometres from the Île Saint-Louis but a world away socially and culturally, the Parc de la Villette lies up against the Boulevard Périphérique. With its wide-open spaces and its whimsical architectural and landscape features, it's popular both with Parisians and with foreign tourists, and one of relatively few places where they coincide. To see the family groups among the crowds relaxing here on a weekend afternoon is to be reminded that Paris today is a multi-ethnic, multicultural city – and a comparatively young one demographically.

PARC DE LA VILLETTE, CITÉ DES SCIENCES ET DE L'INDUSTRIE

XIXe Arrondissement

Europe's biggest science museum simply had to be in France: no other country takes so much pride – or interest – in technology. In the 1970s President Valéry Giscard d'Estaing gave the order for an abandoned abattoir complex out at Villette to be redeveloped: the Cité des Sciences was opened in 1986. Reflecting pools and channels, coloured domes and garden features reinforce the three themes of water, light and vegetation. A showcase for French knowhow, the 'Science City' is also an important educational facility, drawing school parties from all over France and far beyond.

PARC DES BUTTES CHAUMONT

XIXe Arrondissement

Paris is not exactly famous for its mountains, its lakes or its caves, but all these things are to be found – after some stylized fashion – in the Buttes Chaumont Park. This 60-acre expanse of parkland was opened in the 1860s after the careful landscaping of what had been an old quarry. There are winding walks to be had through woodland glades and gardens; there is a waterfall in an underground grotto, and – a splendid centrepiece – a classical belvedere atop a miniature mountain on a craggy island in a lake.

PÈRE LACHAISE CEMETERY

XXe Arrondissement

Here lie luminaries from Chopin and Oscar Wilde to Édith Piaf and Jim 'The Doors' Morrison. Opened in 1804, Père Lachaise took its name from Louis XIV's personal confessor, who first had the land here set aside for a residence for retired priests. In so far as a cemetery ever could be, Père Lachaise became a sought-after address: rich tombs were built, with sumptuous statuary. But this was also a place of living history: in 1871, 147 Communards made a defiant last stand here.

BOIS DE VINCENNES, PARC FLORAL

XIIe Arrondissement

Vincennes was once a separate town, now it is an eastern suburb of the capital. The Bois de Vincennes is now essentially a city park. In the nineteenth century, it was laid out in the 'English' manner – a stylized rendering of what might have been a natural landscape and what we might call open parkland. This contrasted with the much more regimented French style established in the seventeenth century by André Le Nôtre (seen, for example, in the Jardin des Tuileries, page 24 above).

BOIS DE VINCENNES, LAC DAUMESNIL

XIIe Arrondissement

The Bois de Vincennes has no fewer than four lakes, of which Lac Daumesnil is by far the biggest. The lake is large enough to explore by boat and has two large islands. On one stands a belvedere – a classical allusion of a type popular in landscaping of the time. More surprising is the Bois de Vincennes' own Buddhist temple, built for the International Colonial Exhibition of 1931. The Chateau de Vincennes is not, as might be assumed, a modern folly but a real fortress from the fourteenth century.

PARC DE BERCY

XIIe Arrondissement

The *Maison du Lac* makes an evocative centrepiece to the so-called Romantic Garden, one of three distinct sections of the Parc de Bercy. Directly to the north is what might best be described as a Garden of Gardening, with flowerbeds, a rose garden, vegetable patches, an orchard and an orangery. Beyond that is an open meadow area. The whole complex (which includes *La Cinématique*, the National Cinema Museum, a Fairground Museum and footbridge access to the National Library, across the Seine) was created on the site of some wine warehouses demolished in the 1970s.

PLACE D'ITALIE

XIIIe Arrondissement

A major traffic junction, the Place d'Italie marks the very heart of the thirteenth arrondissement, whose handsome Mairie (town hall) still takes pride of place, though to some extent overshadowed by more modern constructions all around. This district is known for its nightlife now. It was always lively, but in less appealing ways, since this was perhaps the poorest part of Paris; the part which, wrote the great nineteenth-century novelist Balzac, 'leaves most brats at the gate of the Foundling Hospital, which sends most beggars to the poorhouse … most delinquents to the police courts'.

PARC MONTSOURIS

XIVe Arrondissement

In the 1860s, what was then the world's biggest reservoir was built atop this hill in the southernmost part of the city. Water was – and still is – brought here from the River Vanne before being distributed as required. The other side of the hill was landscaped in the English style to make what remains one of Paris's most appealing parks. Water remains well to the fore: the gardens' finest feature is a little lake in what was once a quarry, which in turn feeds artificial streams with a waterfall.

A LA
DEFENSE NATIONALE
1870 - 1871

LION OF BELFORT AT PLACE DENFERT-ROCHEREAU

XIVe Arrondissement

The original Denfert-Rochereau was Pierre Philippe, the general of that name. In 1870–71 he organized the successful defence of the north-eastern city of Belfort against a Prussian siege, winning fame and the nickname 'Lion of Belfort'. That name was also given to the massive sandstone lion sculpted by Frédéric Bartholdi, creator of New York's statue of liberty, and placed in Belfort in tribute to that city's courage. That monster stands some 11 m (36 ft) high, despite being carved in a crouched position. The Parisian equivalent, by comparison, is pretty small.

MONTPARNASSE CEMETERY

XIVe Arrondissement

Inevitably, given the age and historic glamour of Père Lachaise, Montparnasse comes a clear second in the cemetery stakes. It's an imposing and atmospheric place, though, its inmates a roll call of modern French history and culture, including composers like César Franck and Camille Saint-Saëns, artists like Chaim Soutine and Man Ray. Philosophers Jean-Paul Sartre and Simone de Beauvoir lie here side by side. There are distinguished French writers like Charles Baudelaire and Guy de Maupassant. Here too is the sociologist Émile Durkheim, the engineer André Citroën, and even the falsely prosecuted 'traitor' Alfred Dreyfus.

TOUR MONTPARNASSE

XVe Arrondissement

Rising 209 m (680 ft) above Montparnasse, this office block was built in the 1970s. There are lovelier sights on the Parisian skyline, but on the other hand there are few more amazing prospects than the panoramic view one gets from the observation platform at the top. From here, you can see the whole city spreading out before you: the Eiffel Tower, the Luxembourg, Les Invalides, the Louvre, Sacré Coeur.... In the almost aerial view you have over the Left Bank in particular, Haussman's nineteenth-century street plan is clear to see.

MUSÉE BOURDELLE

XVe Arrondissement

What was once the house and studio of sculptor Antoine Bourdelle has been a museum since 1949, and Bourdelle himself had made plans for this before his death in 1929. Bourdelle's workspace has been preserved just the way he left it. Here too are his most famous works, and his own (extraordinarily rich and varied) collection of classic French art: not just sculpture (though there are key works by Rodin here), but also paintings by a range of great French artists, including Jean Auguste Dominique Ingres and Eugène Delacroix.

LA VIE DES SCULPTURES
PLAN SUPERFICIEL EST UN
INCIDENT
AIS UN PLAN PROFOND,
CONSTRUCTIF EST UNE
DESTINEE

PARC GEORGES BRASSENS

XVe Arrondissement

Georges Brassens (1921–81), a popular poet and singer, was also a lifelong anarchist, though his was never a voice for violent revolution. He endeared himself with his countrymen and countrywomen by his good-humoured irreverence towards officialdom and his gentle rebelliousness against France's authoritarian tendencies. Brassens composed a famous paean to the public bench as a place for lovers to gaze into one another's eyes and imagine new worlds; to kiss and change each other's lives. So it's appropriate that he should be commemorated by a park.

BOIS DE BOULOGNE, LE PARC DE BAGATELLE

XVIe Arrondissement

A bagatelle is a trinket, a trivial thing. This little park-within-a-park is none of those things, but was created in that trifling sort of spirit. Marie Antoinette bet her brother-in-law the Comte d'Artois that he couldn't build a chateau here in three months: he won, with time to spare. Sixty-three days can seldom have been more productively employed, as this lovely little lodge is small, admittedly, but beautifully designed (by François-Joseph Bélanger) and built. The grounds, now a botanical garden, are a real treasure.

LA GRANDE ARCHE DE LA DÉFENSE

Puteaux, beyond the XVIe and XVIIe Arrondissements

A self-consciously postmodern monument – all shining surface and no substantial core – the Grande Arche still makes an impressive spectacle. The central attraction of a new forward-looking business quarter built just outside the *Périphérique*, it stands strikingly as a symbol for France's future. At the same time, it is subtly integrated with the country's and Paris's past: the Arche represents the end of a historical axis which leads from the Louvre up the Champs Élysées to the Arc de Triomphe then continues along the Avenue Charles de Gaulle.

QUARTIER LATIN AND SAINT GERMAIN-DES-PRÉS

La Rive Gauche isn't just a geographical description: the Left Bank is as much a state of mind, a set of attitudes, a style – sophisticated, sceptical, self-consciously intellectual and artistic. It would, of course, be a ludicrous exaggeration to suggest that these qualities are unique to the area of Paris immediately to the south of the Seine, yet there's little doubt that in *arrondissements* V and VI they seem to set the tone, to hold sway in a way they never quite do elsewhere.

Students sit out at café tables, cigarettes smoking and the coffee strong, discussing everything from Arabic poetry to Marxist theory. Scruffy scholars browse among the paperbacks at pavement bookstalls; well-heeled connoisseurs collect rare volumes; there are contemporary jazz-clubs and avant-garde galleries.... Even now, this is a place that cares passionately about ideas and culture. The life of the Left Bank is the life of the mind. But the real world intrudes and always has done – with its palaces and parliament buildings. The schools and colleges here trained the administrators of France. However hard it has tried to remain aloof, this part of Paris has never been half so remote or sequestered as it might seem.

INSTITUT DU MONDE ARABE

Ve Arrondissement

The Arab World Institute was opened in 1981 to foster understanding between the West and the Arab countries. The Prophet Muhammad discouraged his followers from flaunting their wealth with gold, silver and jewels, so Arab craftsmen found ways (like marquetry, mosaic and the most delicate woodwork and leatherwork) of making ordinary materials precious. In Jean Nouvel's innovative building, these values become architectural, a basic modern glass-and-aluminium construction given an alabaster sheen. What at first glance look to be blank office-block windows are ornamented with lattice-like motifs. These adjust themselves automatically, controlling light levels inside.

JARDIN DES PLANTES

Ve Arrondissement

Paris's main botanical garden occupies almost 30 ha (70 acres) right on the Left Bank of the River Seine. A delightful place to walk and relax in the heart of the city, the Jardin des Plantes is at the same time an open-air laboratory for horticultural study. Scientists here have collected plants and seeds of several thousand different species, many of them rare. The garden has a designated area for Alpine plants and various hothouses for tropical species, plus a number of natural science museums, most notably the Grande Galerie de l'Évolution.

PALAEONTOLOGY MUSEUM

Ve Arrondissement

Walk with dinosaurs in this splendid museum, laid out in an old-fashioned style and on a lavish scale. Opened in 1898, the Galerie de Paléontologie et d'Anatomie Comparée comprises a collection of over a thousand complete skeletons, with innumerable bone fragments and fossils. The presentational values are Victorian, in a good way. Most modern museums have done their best to cut down their glass-case count and incorporate sound and image effects; this collection has become exceptional in paying tribute to the great adventurer-collectors of the nineteenth century.

MUSÉUM NATIONAL D'HISTOIRE NATURELLE

Ve Arrondissement

The National Museum of Natural History has branches across Paris – and, indeed, across the whole of France – but its headquarters is right here, in the beautiful surroundings of the Jardin des Plantes. In some shape or form, the National Museum has existed since the seventeenth century, but its function has changed significantly over time. Once a nursery for the royal gardens – and a resource for the king's apothecaries – it became more scientific in its focus in the nineteenth century. Today, the emphasis is on education, more specifically, on eco-consciousness and climate change.

PARIS MOSQUE

Ve Arrondissement

France's colonial adventures in North Africa were to leave a difficult legacy: first, in the 1950s, in a vicious war in Algeria; more recently, in immigration issues and racial tension. Founded in the 1920s, the Mosquée de Paris predates these problems. Whilst relatively discreet in its design, especially on the outside, it is an open celebration of Islam and its beliefs. In terms of aesthetics, the mosque acknowledges its situation in Europe by being built in the *mudéjar* style developed by the Muslim Moors in Spain, with lovely landscaped gardens and water pools.

LUTETIA AMPHITHEATRE

Ve Arrondissement

Julius Caesar's conquest of Gaul made the country's Celts a subject people, and the Parisii were no exception. Their settlement, called Lutetia by the Romans, was completely redeveloped, with all the civilized amenities of the Roman world. This particular phase of Paris's past has been all but completely expunged by 2000 years of razing and rebuilding, but researchers have been uncovering traces in recent years. The most notable is the Arènes de Lutèce, the remains of a large amphitheatre, uncovered in the nineteenth century, appropriately enough in the Latin Quarter.

ÉGLISE SAINT-ÉTIENNE-DU-MONT

Ve Arrondissement

There has been a chapel here since the sixth century, part of the old Abbey of Saint Geneviève. It became St Étienne's in the thirteenth century and was rebuilt in the sixteenth. The association with Saint Geneviève continued (her tomb is here) and, given her status as patron saint of Paris, St Étienne's has been an important centre for ceremonial processions and pilgrimage. The church also holds the tombs of the seventeenth-century tragedian Jean Racine and mathematician Blaise Pascal. The revolutionary Jean-Paul Marat is buried in the churchyard just outside.

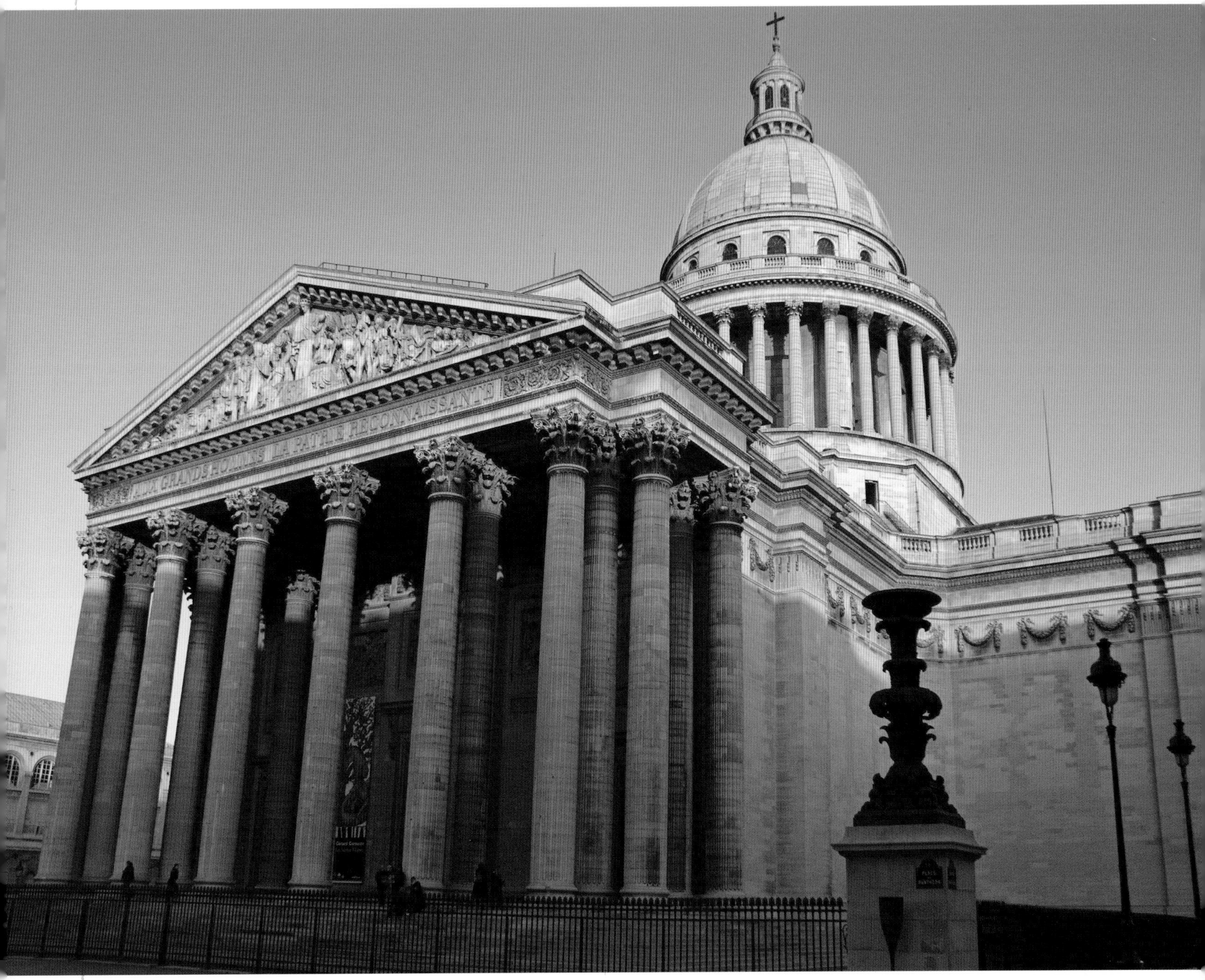
GRANDS HOMMES LA PATRIE RECONNAISSANTE

THE PANTHÉON

Ve Arrondissement

First planned to commemorate Saint Geneviève, Paris's patron saint, this vast and imposing edifice was built between 1758 and 1790 in the Neoclassical style that was then in vogue. Its façade was based on that of the Pantheon in Rome. Though the work of the monarchy, the Panthéon's style suited a Revolutionary regime which looked back admiringly to the early republican days of Roman history. This secular shrine became the burial place for the heroes of the new France, men like Voltaire, Victor Hugo, Émile Zola and many more.

THE SORBONNE

Ve Arrondissement

The name 'Sorbonne' is often used for Paris's ancient university as a whole. Strictly speaking, it's just the college we see here. Founded in 1257 as a theological college, its present building dates from the seventeenth century. Religious teaching wasn't encouraged by the Revolutionary regime and the Sorbonne was shut down. However, in 1808 Napoleon I reopened it as a place of secular learning. So it has remained, revered as one of the world's most prestigious academic institutions and, despite its antiquity, a place of innovation and forward thinking.

MUSÉE DE CLUNY

Ve Arrondissement

The famous Cluny Abbey was in Saône-et-Loire, but the abbot had his Parisian *pied-à-terre* on the Left Bank. This fifteenth-century residence was constructed on still earlier foundations: the Roman baths here have now been opened up to public view. Since 1833, the Hôtel de Cluny itself has also been open as a museum, in this case dedicated to the arts and culture of the medieval age. Though it's full of beautiful and fascinating artefacts, its central attraction is undoubtedly the fifteenth-century tapestry cycle, *The Lady and the Unicorn.*

ÉGLISE SAINT-SÉVERIN

Ve Arrondissement

This church was begun in the eleventh century, but not completed for the best part of 400 years. In its final form, it's a magnificent example of the late-Gothic style. Yet, whilst the exterior boasts a fine collection of finely fashioned gargoyles and other statuary, it's the inside that makes Saint Séverin so unique: the sumptuous stonework of the columns is astounding, the vaulting takes the breath away, the stained glass is awe-inspiring, the eerie light that filters through it enough to make the sightseer's hair stand on end.

ÉGLISE SAINT-JULIEN-LE-PAUVRE

Ve Arrondissement

This church is among the oldest in Paris – there may well have been a chapel of some sort here in the sixth century. The present building was constructed in the 1160s, in the Gothic style. It was dedicated to St Julian the Hospitaller, who dedicated his life to the succour of the poor after pagan witches tricked him into killing his own parents. The church is seen here from René Viviani Square, which has a fountain in the centre created by George Jeancios in 1995. It represents St Julian about his ministry.

FONTAINE SAINT-MICHEL

Ve Arrondissement

An imposing portal to the Latin Quarter for those who come across the bridge from the Île de la Cité, the Place Saint-Michel is dominated by an impressive fountain. This is dominated in its turn by Gabriel Davioud's statue of Michael the Archangel. This famous monument was built by Napoleon III in honour of his uncle: Napoleon I at his most commanding was to have stood here. That proved politically difficult, however, and it was decided that, if the great Bonaparte was not acceptable, the archangel would be the next best thing.

JARDIN DU LUXEMBOURG . FONTAINE DE MÉDICIS

VIe Arrondissement

The Luxembourg Palace was built on the orders of Marie de Médicis, the Italian-born consort of King Henri IV. After Henri's assassination in 1610, Marie ruled France as regent until her son Louis XIII reached majority in 1617, at which point she handed him the reins. For a while she was still a power behind the throne. However, plotted against by Louis' chief minister Cardinal Richelieu, she was sent into exile. She died in obscurity, but has her monument in this palace, these magnificent gardens and this delightful fountain.

JARDIN DU LUXEMBOURG . FOUNTAINE DE L'OBSERVATOIRE

VIe Arrondissement

Even royal palaces and their grounds came under Georges-Eugène Haussmann's critical scrutiny. The Jardin du Luxembourg was no exception. Not that we have much cause to complain. The existing garden was incorporated into a stately avenue linking the old palace with the Paris Observatory. Designed by Jean-Baptiste Carpeaux and dedicated in 1874, this new fountain was to be a focal point. At its centre, four female nudes representing Europe, Asia, Africa and the Americas hold up the sphere of the world above their heads. Emmanuel Frémiet created the rearing horses.

PALAIS DU LUXEMBOURG

VIe Arrondissement

This elegant residence was built at the behest of Marie de Médicis, Henri IV's queen, who wanted something in the Italian style. More specifically, she wanted something to remind her of Florence's fifteenth-century Pitti Palace, her birthplace and the Médicis' ancestral home. The Luxembourg conforms closely to its Italian model in its broad outline, but is seventeenth-century in its Baroque detail. Since the Revolution, the Luxembourg has largely served as a centre of government, having been the seat of the French Senate since the early nineteenth century.

PLACE SAINT-SULPICE

VIe Arrondissement

Not one, not two, not three but four bishops bedeck the fountain at the centre of this handsome square. In their day, they were famous for their oratory, though they had little else in common. One (François Fénelon) was a notorious radical and another (Jacques-Bénigne Bossuet) a defender of the divine right of kings. But the dominant presence here is that of Saint Sulpice's Church, whose austere façade (1732), with its Classical columns, was designed by Giovanni Niccolò Servandoni at a time when others were favouring the architectural frills and furbelows of the Rococo style.

CAFÉ LES DEUX MAGOTS

VIe Arrondissement

If you want the ultimate Paris experience, you may think of walking along the Champs Élysées, or scaling the Eiffel Tower or gawping at Notre Dame. Mais non. Instead, simply sit down at a table at your nearest pavement café. Any café will do, but the one with the most illustrious pedigree is probably Les Deux Magots in Saint Germain-des-Prés. Here you can sip your coffee in the same place as the philosophers Jean-Paul Sartre and Simone de Beauvoir. Fellow-writers Albert Camus and Ernest Hemingway also came here.

Café de Flore
CAFE DE FLORE

CAFÉ DE FLORE

VIe Arrondissement

Intellectuals are nothing if not contrary – or fashion-conscious. The very fact of Les Deux Magots' success marked it down for disdain among the movers and shakers on Paris's literary and artistic scene. The Café de Flore had enjoyed a period of prominence in the early years of the twentieth century during which it was haunted by the Surrealist circle led by André Breton and Guillaume Apollinaire. So when, in the 1970s, Les Deux Magots started to seem too much of a 'tourist trap', the Café de Flore was poised to take its place.

DECORATIVE PORTICO, SQUARE FÉLIX DESRUELLES

VIe Arrondissement

'Sèvres', reads the sign above the arch in this ceramic portico – a minor masterpiece of Art Nouveau. Made by the world-famous *Manufacture nationale* in the south-western suburb of Sèvres, it was originally intended as an entrance to the Universal Exposition of 1900. Architect Charles Risler and sculptor Jules Coutan collaborated on this work. At its centre a young woman sits and looks out with a self-confident – almost challenging – air. Now merely decorative, the portico stands against the wall in the garden of this little square beside the Church of Saint Germain-des-Prés.

COUR DU COMMERCE SAINT-ANDRÉ

VIe Arrondissement

Lined as it is with boutiques, bistros and cafés, this little passage bustles with life and brims with sometimes sensational, sometimes macabre history. Here it was, for example, that in 1789, Jean-Paul Marat wrote and published his rabble-rousing newspaper, *L'Ami du Peuple*. Here his fellow-revolutionary Georges Danton had his digs. Danton was to die on the guillotine and, ironically, it was in the Cour du Commerce Saint-André that Dr Guillotin had his first prototype made, having it tested on sheep and calves.

INSTITUT DE FRANCE

VIe Arrondissement

The Institut de France was founded in 1795 as an umbrella organization for a number of societies. These included everything from the Académie française (which had been established in 1635 to oversee standards in French language) to the Académie des Beaux Arts. National academies exist elsewhere, of course. In France they loom larger than in the Anglo-Saxon countries, and have historically played a more prescriptive role in fixing what is 'correct'. The Institut occupies a converted college, built in 1691 to a design by Louis XIV's favourite architect, Louis Le Vau.

PONT DES ARTS

VIe Arrondissement

This famous metal footbridge spans the Seine, linking the Louvre with the Institut de France, but it's also an important attraction in its own right. Artists and tourists have always come here for the views but, in recent years, it's also been a destination for lovers. Couples come here to canoodle; to enjoy the twilight hours of the world's most romantic city. Then they use little padlocks to pledge their undying love. Attaching them carefully to the railing, they cast the key into the river below. They're then symbolically and eternally locked together.

EIFFEL TOWER AND AROUND

Approximately 30 million foreigners come to the world's most-visited city each year. They come to take in the tourist sights, of course, but they also come for more particular purposes – everything from fashion weeks to film festivals and sports events. By and large these don't disappoint. Paris loves to put on a show and takes its established duty to wow the world extremely seriously.

The city is quite simply Exposition mad: it staged no fewer than five World's Fairs in the nineteenth century alone. The Exposition Internationale des Arts Décoratifs et Industriels Modernes of 1925 inaugurated an important aesthetic movement in Art Deco which is recognizable, and influential, to this day. An unmistakable icon, representing Paris as a whole, the Eiffel Tower is more specifically suggestive of these exhibitionistic tendencies: built for the World's Fair of 1889, it's a temporary structure that simply stayed. This aspect of Paris is also to be seen across the Pont d'Iéna in what are now historic monuments like the Trocadéro, but it's also to be seen in earlier, more obviously permanent, structures too. The spectacular appearance of Les Invalides, the École Militaire and the Parc du Champ de Mars indicate that the desire to impress goes very deep.

Musée d'Orsay Clock

VIIe Arrondissement

Now a world-famous art museum, with a stunning collection of Impressionist and Post-Impressionist paintings and modern sculpture, the Musée d'Orsay was originally an exhibit in itself. The Gare d'Orsay railway station was opened for the Universal Exposition of 1900, and served south-western France until the start of the Second World War. After that it became a terminus for suburban trains, before being more or less mothballed for several years. The Musée d'Orsay stands on the banks of the Seine, its clock clearly visible across the river, one of Paris's most striking landmarks.

Port des Champs-Élysées

VIIIe Arrondissement

At various points along the Seine in Paris, there are quays for riverboats and barges. One of the most famous is the Port des Champs-Élysées. Running, roughly, between the Alexandre III and the Invalides bridges, it's an important terminus for tourist trips. Increasingly, though, the Port has become a destination in its own right: people come here for the fabulous views it affords across the River. And in the evenings they come to dance and have fun at Le Showcase, a vast nightclub built in converted boatsheds on the quay.

LA BRIGANTINE
NE-O-VENT

PONT ALEXANDRE III

VIIe Arrondissement

This exuberantly ornamented bridge was one of a complex of works built to beautify the city in time for the Universal Expo of 1900. The Gare (now the Musée) d'Orsay was another; so too was the Grand Palais, whose extravagant appearance echoes that of the bridge by which it stands. The Pont Alexandre III was named in honour of the Russian tsar who had signed a peace treaty with Napoleon III a few years before, in 1892. It is decorated with the symbols of imperial Russia and the French Republic.

ASSEMBLEE NATIONALE
INVALIDES

PALAIS BOURBON

VIIe Arrondissement

Directly across the river from the Place de la Concorde stands this impressive pile, named for a ruling dynasty but the seat of French democracy for over 200 years. It was built for one of Louis XIV's daughters, but was taken over after the Revolution and became the meeting place for the 'Council of 500'. It subsequently became the permanent home for the National Assembly. Just as this legislative function was thrust upon a royal residence, so too a Classical portico – suggestive of ancient republican rule – was imposed upon the earlier design.

BASILIQUE SAINTE-CLOTILDE

VIIe Arrondissement

With Notre Dame, Sainte-Chapelle, Saint-Séverin and more, Paris boasts several of the world's great Gothic churches. But it also has important examples of the Gothic Revival style. The first of these was this beautiful basilica built in 1846–57 to a design by German-born architect Franz Christian Gau. The Gothic style had long been viewed as barbaric, but between the Romantic rejection of Classical order and symmetry and a new appreciation of the workmanship and the individualism involved in the medieval style, it was rediscovered and became a craze.

LES INVALIDES

VIIe Arrondissement

L'Hôtel National des Invalides was built by Louis XIV as a veterans' hospital. Napoleon subsequently co-opted it as a shrine to himself. Given France's contributions to culture and to gracious living, it's easily forgotten how long (and how violently) it dominated Western Europe. Louis XIV, the Sun King, didn't just build spectacular palaces. Seventy-six per cent of his state budget went into military expenditure and by 1700 two per cent of France's population were under arms. A hundred years later, Napoleon was rampaging across Europe. He was buried at Les Invalides after his death.

CHURCH OF THE DOME, LES INVALIDES

VIIe Arrondissement

Libéral Bruant designed Les Invalides, but he was helped by Hardouin-Mansart, and his assistant's contribution came to dominate the complex as a whole. The gigantic dome, which towers to a height of 107 m (350 ft), was based on that of St Peter's Basilica in Rome, and almost matches it, in beauty and in scale. Below are buried France's military heroes, most notably Napoleon I. A smaller chapel, dedicated to St Louis, was built for daily use by the hospital's inmates, many of whom lived here long term as retirees.

MUSÉE RODIN

VIIe Arrondissement

The sometime Hôtel Biron seems much too grand to have been a sculptor's studio, but Auguste Rodin made many of his masterpieces here, where he rented a few rooms as working space. At the time, in fact, it was semi-derelict and due for demolition. Some of Rodin's creations went on to win him worldwide fame, some of which you can see here: works like *The Kiss* (1889) and *The Thinker* (1902). By 1909 he had persuaded the government to purchase the house and transform it into a museum of his work.

LA PAGODE

VIIe Arrondissement

Apparently a Chinese temple in the very heart of Paris, the Pagoda is in fact a picture-house. A twentieth-century folly, it was built by a director of the nearby department store Le Bon Marché as a present for his wife. As if its pagoda-like appearance was not exotic enough, its façade is festooned with hanging plants and it has a lush green garden, as well as a famous Japanese Room inside. In a city of sophisticated cinemas, La Pagode stands out with its programme of art movies from around the world.

HÔTEL MATIGNON

VIIe Arrondissement

The Hôtel Matignon was built in 1725. After the Revolution it was sold and for a while the famous diplomat Talleyrand lived here. In this house he had his friends – and enemies – to dinner and, in between courses, decided the fate of nations. As accomplished in domestic as foreign diplomacy, he served Louis XVI, the Revolutionaries, the Emperor Napoleon I and the restored monarchy in succession, becoming one of the most prominent figures of his age, respected and reviled in equal measure. The Hôtel has been the Prime Minister's official residence since the 1950s.

ÉCOLE MILITAIRE

VIIe Arrondissement

The teenage Napoleon Bonaparte was sworn in here in 1784 and graduated just a year later. 'He will go far,' said his examiner's report. And in a certain sense he did, of course, although his body was ultimately laid to rest less than a kilometre away in Les Invalides. The idea of an academy for young officers without independent means originated with Madame de Pompadour, the mistress – and it's said, the real master – of Louis XV. The École opened its doors in 1750 and is educating smart young soldiers to this day.

Champ de Mars

VIIe Arrondissement

With its paths and ornamental pool, this vast open area just about passes muster as a park. Primarily, though, it's a place from which to gaze up at the Eiffel Tower. Not that this is a worthless function, by any means. Gustav Eiffel's iconic masterpiece can in some ways be best appreciated from ground level; the sight of it rearing up here is truly awe-inspiring. In the old days, it was used as a space for large-scale military parades – hence its name, the Field of Mars – or as an exhibition ground.

EIFFEL TOWER

VIIe Arrondissement

Constructed from over 7,000 tonnes of wrought iron and for 42 years the world's tallest building, the Eiffel Tower is emblematic not just of Paris but of industrial production. It was of course designed as a totemic centrepiece for the 1889 World's Fair: a celebration of capitalist achievement. Engineered rather than built, it was, said the Marxist intellectual Walter Benjamin, a montage, pieced together from thousands of identical units. Made from iron, the industrial material *par excellence*, it didn't attempt to conceal its constructed nature, but was presented naked, unclothed with wood or masonry.

MUSÉE DU QUAI BRANLY

VIIe Arrondissement

A postmodern home for 'primitive' art, this museum, which opened in 1995, boasts one of the world's finest collections of indigenous art and craft from around the world. Africa, Asia, Oceania and the Americas are all represented here: over 3,000 artefacts are on display (a quarter of a million more are stored behind the scenes) with video and digital displays about the peoples that produced them. The visitor is guided along a winding path, between the exhibits (and between striking if perplexing leather-upholstered partition units), on a genuine journey of discovery.

29

29 AVENUE RAPP

VIIe Arrondissement

There aren't too many world-famous front doors: London's 10 Downing Street is an obvious one, but that of number 29 Avenue Rapp must run a close second. Not so much an example as an explosion of Art Nouveau, it was designed by Jules Lavirotte and built in 1901. It won him a major prize, as, three years later, did his so-called Ceramic Hotel not far away in Avenue de Wagram. Glazed tiles were used there to add a sheen of luxury and glamour. The result is more confection than construction.

ZOUAVE ON THE PONT DE L'ALMA

VIIIe Arrondissement

The *zouaves* of the French Army were light infantrymen of Algerian origin. Fast and mobile, they were also tough and fierce. They fought in many key campaigns, including the Crimean War of 1853–56, where they played a part in the allied victory at Alma. Hence this statue underneath the bridge erected in commemoration of the battle. When the Seine floods, the *zouave*'s feet get wet. When the water reaches his knees, it's understood by all on the river that the level is too high for safe navigation.

PALAIS DE TOKYO

XVIe Arrondissement

This important museum of contemporary art was built for the International Exhibition of Arts and Technology of 1937. It has no real connection with Japan beyond the fact that the street that separates it from the Seine (now the Avenue de New York) was, for a few decades, called the Avenue de Tokyo. The centre of a lively scene, the Palais doesn't just display art, it participates in its creation – and invites the public to – at its own creative laboratory, the Pavillon Neuflize OBC, which opened in 2001.

PALAIS GALLIERA

XVIe Arrondissement

In the 1880s, the Duchess of Galliera decided to house her family's considerable collection of art and furniture in this splendid purpose-built museum and leave it all to the French nation. As relations worsened between the Third Republic and descendants of the *Ancien Régime*, however, she changed her mind and bequeathed it all elsewhere. She did leave the palais to the city of Paris, though, and it was made into the Musée de la Mode et du Costume, with exhibitions recording developments in fashion from as far back as the eighteenth century.

Galliera
Henry Clarke / Cadolle, 1957
© Galliera
G

PALAIS DE CHAILLOT

XVIe Arrondissement

Paris has had so many world's fairs that it's possible to imagine an Expo-archeology. What was once the village of Chaillot was redeveloped for the 1867 World's Fair. This was built over with a brand new Palais du Trocadéro (named for an 1823 victory over Spain) for another world's fair just 11 years later. It was all pulled down to make way for the present Palais de Chaillot at the time of the Exposition Internationale of 1937. There are museums of naval history, architecture and anthropology at what is widely known as the Trocadéro.

JARDINS DU TROCADÉRO

XVIe Arrondissement

Light and water play in counterpoint in the Fountain of Warsaw as seen by night – so much water that we hardly need the Seine. The river disappears altogether in the view across to the Eiffel Tower at the heart of what might be called the city's Exposition Quarter. The Fountain, created for the Universal Expo of 1937, is actually a collection of fountains, spraying water in co-ordinated jets around and over a series of interconnecting basins and cascades. It is the spectacular centrepiece to an impressive formal garden.

PONT DE BIR-HAKEIM

XV and XVIe Arrondissements

Saint Joan of Arc careens into action, representing *La France Renaissante* (France Reborn), as imagined by the Danish sculptor Holger Wendekinch and donated by the Danish community of Paris. The statue stands in a little garden atop a pier that juts out from the central support of the Pont de Bir-Hakeim and can be reached by the pedestrian walkway that occupies the lower level of this double-decker bridge. The Métro runs along the upper level. The bridge was named for a battle fought by the Free French in North Africa in 1942.

ÎLE AUX CYGNES

XV and XVIe Arrondissements

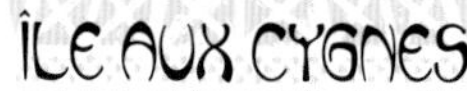

The real Island of the Swans is no longer an island, and hasn't been since the eighteenth century, when the channel on its southern side was filled. In 1827, however, an artificial Île aux Cygnes was created. This has striking statues at either end: upstream there's Holger Wendekinch's dashing Joan of Arc; downstream, looking west, is a quarter-scale Statue of Liberty. The New York statue was of course given to the people of America by those of France – a gift from the revolutionaries of 1789 to those of 1776.

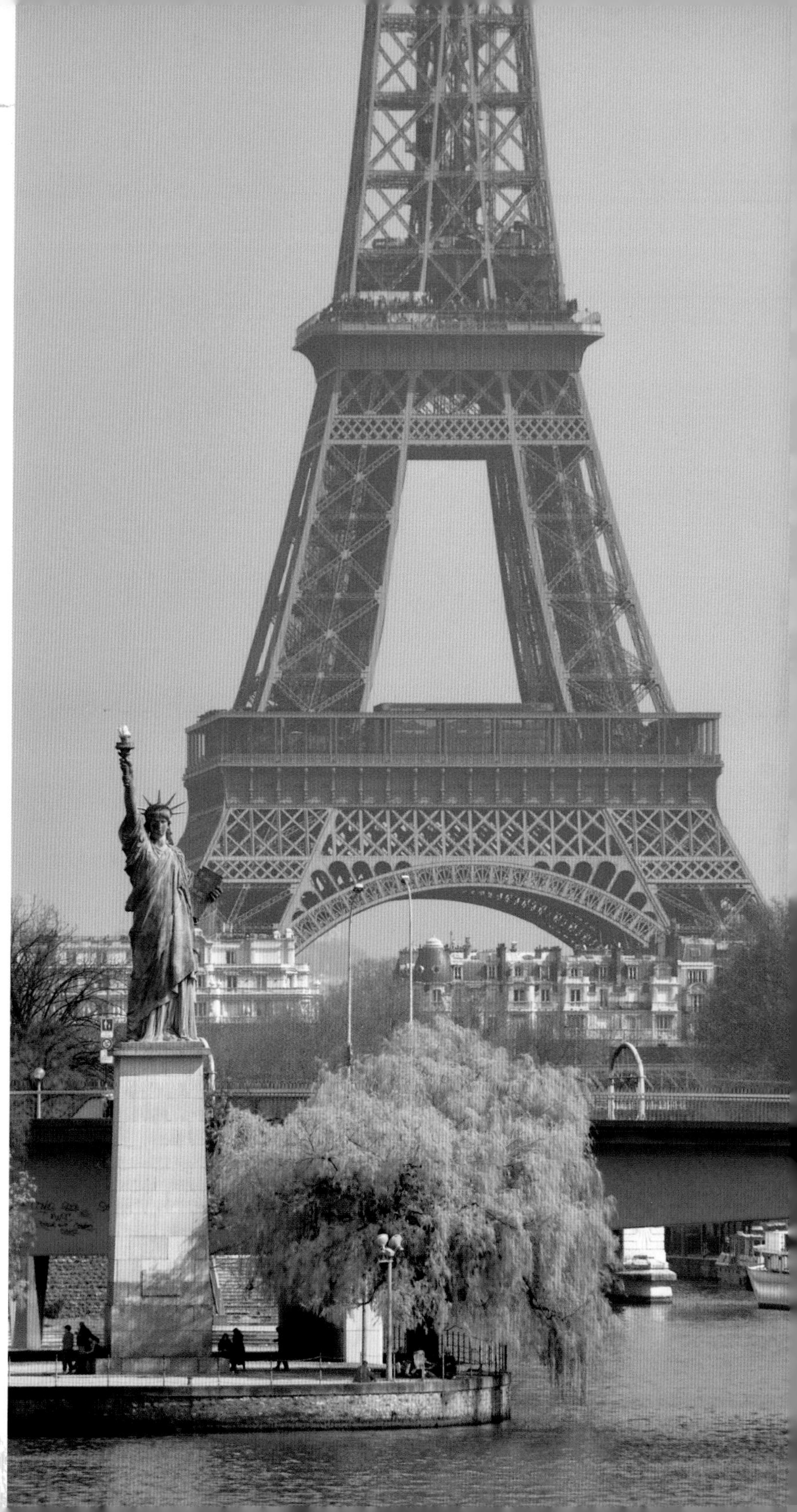

MUSÉE MARMOTTAN-MONET

XVIe Arrondissement

This was once the townhouse of the wealthy collector and scholar Paul Marmottan. He left it to the Académie des Beaux Arts on his death. Since it opened as a museum in the 1930s, what was already a fine collection of paintings, sculptures and furniture from the First Empire period has been supplemented by a series of bequests. These have tilted it towards a focus on French nineteenth-century art, particularly that of the Impressionists. Some of Monet's most important works are to be found here, as are masterpieces by Gauguin and Renoir.

MONTMARTRE
MOULIN ROUGE
MAGGI
LE CONSULAT
LE CONSULAT

MONTMARTRE AND BEYOND

Bohemia was of course a country – what we now call the Czech Republic – but it was also a sensibility, a state of mind. France's first Bohemians were Roma, vaguely believed to have hailed from Central Europe (English tradition accorded them Egyptian origins as 'Gypsies').

From the nineteenth century, however, the term was – more or less disdainfully – applied to a growing community of footloose artists, writers and musicians because, in the eyes of respectable society, they drifted without direction through the world. As the middle class consolidated its position at the centre of French society, such an easy-going lifestyle was marginalized. This took place both literally and physically, when Baron Haussmann's improvements cleared away the wilder slums and the more anarchic residential quarters. The Bohemians were displaced into the outer suburbs. Some moved south to Montparnasse; others moved north to the hilly slopes above the city, at the time an industrial quarter, with quarries, a poor population and rather too many squalid drinking dens. It also had several working windmills. The story of how one of these eventually became a celebrated cabaret club, renowned around the world, tells the story of modern Montmartre itself.

MONTMARTRE CEMETERY

XVIIIe Arrondissement

The Bohemians weren't the only ones to be relegated to the margins in nineteenth-century Paris. As in London – such as in Highgate or Kensal Green – so too were cemeteries. The old churchyard burial grounds were bursting, and with bourgeois tastes craving space and statuary, cemeteries sprang up, from Père Lachaise to Montparnasse. Montmartre's cemetery is tucked away in an old quarry. As might be expected, it has become a posthumous home to a host of celebrated writers, artists and musicians, from Dumas and Degas to Delibes and Berlioz.

MOULIN ROUGE

IX and XVIIIe Arrondissements

Today it's one of the world's top tourist draws with convoys of coaches lining the street outside, but it would be churlish to suggest that the Moulin Rouge had been 'spoiled'. The prices are high, of course. The entertainment, once so shocking, now seems naïve. Yet it's still undoubtedly an experience and a half. With its warm, red, fin-de-siècle décor and its glowing glass light-fittings, the interior is as atmospheric as it was the night the band struck up for the first can-can in the 1890s.

MOULIN ROUGE
BAL
DU
ULIN ROUG

MUSÉE DE LA VIE ROMANTIQUE

IXe Arrondissement

'Romantic' isn't the word that springs to mind as you walk down the Boulevard de Clichy in Pigalle, a place of sex shops and the sleazier sort of cabaret. A few streets to the south, however, is a quieter quarter, with narrow streets and lovely old houses – like number 16 rue Chaptal. This delightful pavilion with its cobbled courtyard and little garden was owned by the artist Ary Scheffer, who hosted a famous salon here. It is now a museum devoted to the memory of Chopin's lover, the writer Lucile Aurore Dupin or George Sand.

Musée
Collections permanentes
Thé dans le jardin
→

METROPOLITAIN
ABBESSES

PLACE DES ABBESSES

XVIIIe Arrondissement

The Métro is more than a rapid-transit system: it's a Paris institution, a lifestyle choice, a cultural phenomenon and, most of all, an advertisement for the elegantly quirky aesthetic of Art Nouveau. Even so, the station in the Place des Abbesses stands out. It's one of only three in Paris with an original entrance designed by Hector Guimard (1867–1942). Like the other founders of Art Nouveau, Guimard had the hope that artistic beauty might be mass-produced, for all to enjoy. The Paris Métro was perhaps its greatest triumph.

JE T'AIME WALL

XVIIIe Arrondissement

Just off Abbesses is the Square Jehan Rictus, named for a poet, but now more famous for those three little words. Here, in a romantic garden, you can stand before a wall on which more than a thousand 'I love you's can be read. From 1992, musician Frédéric Baron wandered Paris with a notebook, asking friends and neighbours and stopping strangers, assembling declarations in 300 languages. With the help of calligrapher Claire Kito, he transferred them to more than 600 ceramic tiles, which were then mounted on this very special wall.

PLACE DU TERTRE

XVIIIe Arrondissement

'Do you remember that spring?…/Those long and tender twilights,/Like the cry of a train to the north?/You know, when we were going to dine/beneath the trees, in the Place du Tertre?' Jules Romains' recollections, in the song 'The Lovers' Voyage' (1920), are sentiments shared by countless other visitors to this lovely little square. This is Montmartre's focal point. Maurice Utrillo and Pablo Picasso lived here; Salvador Dalí was around the corner. They're long gone, of course, but the twilights are just as tender, and to this day you can dine beneath the trees.

RUE FOYATIER

XVIIIe Arrondissement

Not so much a street as a staircase, the rue Foyatier connects the rue Tardieu with the rue Saint-Eleuthère, running directly up and down the steep hillside to the Sacré-Coeur Basilica. A funicular railway alongside the street makes the ascent much easier, or you can brave the crowds (and the crowds of souvenir sellers) and climb the landscaped pathways via the Square Villette. Though it seems to have been conjured into existence to serve Sacré-Coeur, the rue Foyatier actually predates it by several years, having been created as early as 1867.

BASILIQUE DU SACRÉ-COEUR

XVIIIe Arrondissement

This splendid church was begun in 1873, after France's defeat in the Franco-Prussian War and the suppression of the Paris Commune (1871). It was built in commemoration of those who gave their lives in the former and in penance for the latter, though the Communards themselves were not consulted. Montmartre had been a centre of sedition: the insurgents had even marshalled cannon on the heights to bombard the city. So placing Sacré-Coeur up there was also a way of symbolically reclaiming Montmartre and restoring conservative order.

PARC DE LA TURLURE

XVIIIe Arrondissement

This park offers a wonderful close-up view of the Basilica de Sacré-Coeur. Built in dazzling white Travertine limestone, the Basilica's form is highly distinctive; Paul Abadie's design is Byzantine in inspiration. Striking as it is externally, the interior is arguably even more compelling. There are some stunning mosaics, but overall the mood is of restraint and a spiritual calm reigns. Though construction began in 1871, the Basilica was not completed until 1917, by which time France was embroiled in the First World War and consecration had to wait.

MUSÉE DE MONTMARTRE

XVIIIe Arrondissement

Montmartre as we know it is relatively new, built in the aftermath of Haussmann's great improvement scheme. The Hôtel de Rosimond stands out, having been built in the seventeenth century. It takes its name from an early owner – Rosimond was the stage name of Claude de la Rose, who took Molière's place in his company's productions after the great playwright died in 1673. Where better to have a museum recording the history of old Montmartre, its colonization by artists, writers and musicians and its transformation into the capital of Bohemia?

PETIT TRAIN DE MONTMARTRE

XVIIIe Arrondissement

Calling at Place Blanche, the Moulin Rouge, the Cemetery, Sacré-Coeur … and, in short, all the main attractions in Montmartre, the Little Train takes just under 40 minutes to complete its tour. The *butte* may not be much of a mountain by Alpine standards – only 130 m (420 ft) – but, as anyone who's just made the climb will tell you, it's seriously steep. To explore it properly, moreover, means more schlepping, up and down and along narrow and winding streets. It can all get quite taxing in the summer heat.

MOULIN DE LA GALETTE

XVIIIe Arrondissement

There's been a windmill here since as long ago as the seventeenth century. By the nineteenth it was a popular place for drinking and dancing. It has been immortalized by some of the painters who joined the crowds relaxing here, most famously Pierre-Auguste Renoir in 1876. At this stage, it was still a working mill: the galettes (little round loaves) from which it took its name were made from flour produced here. A patron would typically chew on one of these with a glass of wine.

RUE DE L'ABREUVOIR

XVIIIe Arrondissement

This street takes its name from the *abreuvoir*, or trough, which used to stand here, so that the horses and cattle of the community could be watered. The Maison Rose, seen here, is a restaurant, made famous by Maurice Utrillo in a celebrated painting of around 1912. Utrillo was one of many artists living in Montmartre at the time. Unlike the others, however, he was actually born here. So well known did Utrillo's paintings of his home neighbourhood become that it might be said that to some extent we see Montmartre through his eyes.

LA BONNE FRANQUETTE AND LE CONSULAT

XVIIIe Arrondissement

A popular *guinguette* – a cheap eating, drinking and dancing establishment – La Bonne Franquette was a favourite place of Vincent van Gogh in the 1880s. At that time, he and his brother Theo lived round the corner from here in the rue Lepic; they would frequently drop in for a simple meal and a glass of wine. It's believed that this was the *guinguette* depicted in Vincent's famous 1886 painting of that name. Sometimes they rang the changes by going to Le Consulat, across the street. Monet, Toulouse-Lautrec and (later) Picasso also came here.

4
22
LAPIN AGILE
CABARETS

Lapin Agile

XVIIIe Arrondissement

It's hard to imagine how any of Montmartre's artists ever managed to produce a painting – they seem to have spent their lives on an extended café crawl. The Lapin Agile (Agile Rabbit) was another haunt, not just for painters like Utrillo, Modigliani and Picasso (whose painting of the place brought it worldwide fame) but also for the proto-Surrealist poet and novelist Guillaume Apollinaire. The famous sign shows a rabbit hopping out of a cooking pot to safety, and became emblematic of a bohemian community which made a virtue of living by its wits.

Art Nouveau Posters on the Rue des Saules

XVIIIe Arrondissement

The original intention of Art Nouveau was to incorporate organic forms into art and ornamentation – all those swirling tendrils, stalks and leaves. But its practitioners also shared with William Morris's earlier English Arts and Crafts movement and Germany's later Bauhaus the ambition of bringing artistic integrity to industrial design. The poster was an obvious meeting point for the commercial and the artistic impulses, and Art Nouveau ushered in a golden age. Most famous of all is the work of Henri Toulouse-Lautrec (1864–1901) whose representations of Montmartre nightlife are iconic.

ROTONDE DE LA VILLETTE

XIXe Arrondissement

This imposing rotunda is all that survives of the Wall of the Farmers-General, a formidable fortification which once surrounded the whole of Paris. Some 24 km (15 miles) in length, it was built in the 1780s, just before the Revolution. Its purpose was not to keep out attacking armies but to prevent the passage of contraband into the capital. The so-called Farmers-General were not growers of crops or keepers of livestock but freelance tax collectors and customs officers. This function was farmed out to independent operators by the crown.

CANAL SAINT-MARTIN

Xe Arrondissement

Napoleon I ordered the construction of this waterway, which links the River Seine and the Canal de l'Ourcq, and beyond that with the wider canal network. The Emperor wanted a way of bringing fresh drinking water to a city subject to frequent epidemics, and the Canal Saint-Martin served as an aqueduct. At the same time, it was always understood that it would have a major part to play in moving freight. The swing bridge here spans the Bassin des Marais, between the bottom of the Passerelle Alibert and the top of the rue Dieu.

QUAI DE VALMY

Xe Arrondissement

France's canal system, like those of other countries, seemed for a long time to have been superseded by other modes of transportation and was allowed to slide into semi-dereliction. But France has pioneered the push to get goods off the roads and back on to the water and taken steps to restore its waterways. As elsewhere, the possibilities of canal-side developments as an urban environment have been discovered. The old *quais*, pumphouses and warehouse buildings along the Canal Saint-Martin have become the focus for a trendy residential and retail quarter.

Stella Cadente
Stella Cadente

INDEX

Page numbers in *italics* refer to illustrations.